To my grandmother,
Joyce-Ann, who taught me how
to bake with lard, the seasons, and love

To my mother-in-law, Rachel,
who taught me that the presentation is
as important as the recipe

And mostly to my mother, Susan,
who taught me pretty much
everything else

CONTENTS

PREFACE

When I decided to name my company Potluck, my mother immediately thought it was a terrible idea. "Potlucks always have horrible food!" she chided. "You don't want to be associated with something that people dread." I tried to explain to her that it was a metaphor: I wanted to bring everyone to the table, have different ideas come together for one purpose, and showcase a variety of talents. But in a way we were both right. A potluck, a picnic, or any kind of gathering around food can be a wonderful way to bring people together, but only if it is done properly.

Most dinner parties today do not represent the Pinterest-inspired dreams we see online and in magazines. Reality is more often family and friends with some food and a few decent (or not-so-decent) bottles of wine, hoping to enjoy their afternoon or evening. Bringing food from disparate parts is often the solution—maybe the first choice or maybe just the necessity. But the resulting potluck doesn't have to be the nightmare my mother imagined.

How many dinners do we now have where someone says, "What can I bring?" and the host welcomes the offer to bring something substantial like a salad or the dessert? Many dinner parties are a group effort, designed for fun and ease rather than formality. Bringing food is now just part of the modern modern-day dinner scenario.

These recipes are meant to take away the burden of playing host and bring people together around food they want to eat. They are for picnics in the park when you want to make sure you have enough food to stay all day; for neighborly meals delivered to a family that needs a few weeks away from the stove after an illness or a new baby; for that holiday meal no one wants to volunteer to host; for block parties, school gatherings, or study groups; and even (or especially) for a weeknight meal at home. They are for building community around food.

Bring It! is for those perfectionists who don't think "shortcut" is a dirty word. The recipes here are practical, fun, and foolproof and make sense for cooks who don't have access to obscure ingredients or the time to perfect a soufflé. These recipes are, I hope, aspirational *and* attainable, all while holding up beautifully after a jaunt across town.

It's a motto I've come to live by in these busy times. Case in point: a couple of years ago I got involved in a chef conference called Cook It Raw, where some of the world's best chefs come together to learn in a new environment. The conference was being held for the first time in the United States in Charleston, South Carolina, my hometown. I offered to host something at my family home. One thing led to another, and suddenly I was offering to have a casual meal ready as the first stop on this weeklong bonanza. Instead of just attending a conference, I was now also cooking for chefs as acclaimed as Dan Barber, April Bloomfield, and Albert Adria. There was no way my cooking could match their talents. But I knew that after traveling from afar, everyone would probably just want a chance to hang out, and get to know Charleston and its cuisine. I forced myself to relax, and plan a menu that would encourage the guests to relax too.

My task was to make a lot of food and to have it work for the crowd whenever they showed up. I made casual dishes like pimento cheese dip, grits cakes, and oyster shooters. Then I called in the reinforcements of a family friend who makes the world's best deviled eggs. I asked another friend if he could bring along some benne wafers, a sweet and delectable local dish. The dinner was a success. By the end of the week, I had received multiple e-mails from chefs and attendees: despite all the amazing food that the chefs later experienced, that initial, casual introduction to Charleston had been deemed a favorite moment. It allowed them to unwind. Nothing was fussy, and the casual serve-yourself atmosphere allowed people a delicious respite from the rest of the week's frenetic pace. Even among the most illustrious of cooks, a potluck can be the best-case scenario.

I've been lucky to spend many years learning from incredible chefs and eating around the world. But I also know that there's only so much time most of us have to devote to a recipe. This book aims to take those experiences and distill them into relatable, effortless dishes. Just because a recipe is easy doesn't mean it has to feel basic. Just because it took only 20 minutes doesn't mean your dish won't be the hit of the party. I want you to abandon the notion that cooking for guests needs to be complicated to be impressive. Deciding on the menu ahead of time and outsourcing some of your dishes to your dinner guests should no longer be seen as a backup or cheating: it's a smarter way of cooking that we all are aiming to do more of.

It's time to bring it.

Make it and Take it!

If potlucks bring to mind covered dish dinners, it's time to rebrand. Think of them instead as outsourced dinner parties: when everyone brings a dish to share, entertaining is as easy as setting the table. Inside *Bring It!*, you'll find dozens of simple dishes that are perfect for carrying to any occasion. Each recipe includes a note called "How to Bring It," for make-ahead, reheating, and transport instructions, which removes the guesswork from taking it on the go. The 100 recipes are as at home at a dinner with the neighbors as they are at a picnic in the park or school luncheon: Snap Pea Salad with Parmesan and Bacon, Pistachio and Anchovy Pasta, Tahini Lamb and Rice, Cauliflower Gratin, and S'mores Bars. Appetizers, salads, mains, vegetables, and all-important desserts come together easily, hold well, and travel beautifully. They'll have you rethinking the potluck.

bring it!

Tried and True Recipes for Potlucks and Casual Entertaining

ALI ROSEN

PHOTOGRAPHY BY **NOAH FECKS**

RUNNING PRESS
PHILADELPHIA

Running Press
Hachette Book Group
1290 Avenue of the Americas, New York, NY 10104
www.runningpress.com
@Running_Press
Printed in China
First Edition: March 2018

Published by Running Press, an imprint of Perseus Books, LLC, a subsidiary of Hachette Book Group, Inc. The Running Press name and logo is a trademark of the Hachette Book Group.

The Hachette Speakers Bureau provides a wide range of authors for speaking events. To find out more, go to www.hachettespeakersbureau.com or call (866) 376-6591.

The publisher is not responsible for websites (or their content) that are not owned by the publisher.

Photography copyright © 2018 by Noah Fecks
Prop styling by Kristi Hunter
Food styling by Ashton Keefe
Print book cover and interior design by Susan Van Horn

Library of Congress Control Number: 2017955766

ISBNs: 978-0-7624-6272-8 (hardcover), 978-0-7624-6273-5 (ebook)

LREX

10 9 8 7 6 5 4 3 2 1

CHAPTER 1

How to Bring It

There's an art to a meal where all the food is made ahead or brought in. It should be an orchestrated dance of different cooks in different kitchens all coming together at one table for a meal that feels both cohesive and simple. It's a way to include everyone: everyone contributes, everyone is involved, everyone is waiting to hear word that his or her dish is delicious. So how do you ensure that your meal is successful? How do you keep it from being a collection of disparate dishes? It starts by thinking about the event as a whole, before you even get to the food.

the big picture

START WITH A MORE CASUAL MIND-SET

—•—

A meal where dishes are coming from various cooks isn't like a regular dinner, so only plan dishes that can travel well and sit out. If your dish can't be divided easily or served when it is no longer piping hot then don't plan on making it. But don't sacrifice flavor for practicality. Though your dish might be one of many, that doesn't mean it should be boring. Each dish can pack its own punch to make for a delicious meal of surprises.

If you are the host, you can control how the table is set and the food served, but let yourself be as flexible as you can with the planning. Accept that no one else will ever do the same thing you would: that's always a good starting point.

PREPLAN THE FOOD GENERALITIES

—•—

Anytime multiple people are bringing dishes, you can't leave the menu up to chance. Make sure each category is represented so that you don't have ten main dishes and no sides or desserts. Also think about allergies and food preferences: you want everyone to have options in case you wind up with meat eaters, pescatarians, vegans, and gluten-free dieters all in one room (unlucky for you). It also never hurts to ask people for details on their specific restrictions. I once had a dinner party where a guest told me she didn't eat meat, so I assumed she ate fish. When mealtime came she was left without a main course, and it was pretty embarrassing. So while it might seem like overkill, check in with each guest.

LOCATION, LOCATION, LOCATION

———•———

The place where you'll be dining will greatly influence the dish you choose. Want to bring something to a friend who has been in the hospital? Don't assume there is room in the fridge for a huge casserole dish. Planning on an outdoor picnic? Make sure you are bringing a dish that can be cut with a plastic fork and knife. And anytime you need heat, always ask if there will be an oven *and* if it is already in use. Consider the location and setup before you get your heart set on a certain recipe.

KEEP THEMES BROAD

———•———

If you're planning for a lot of people to come together and each bring a dish, remember that it should be about bringing different styles together, not excluding anyone. The more specific your culinary theme is, the harder it might be for your guests. A Super Bowl party or an outdoor picnic are broad enough that everyone can bring something, but a dinner of only Turkish food or casseroles might not bring out the best in your guests. So plan wisely and have a sense of what the other cooks' strengths are.

the practical nitty-gritty

Bringing food requires a few extra things to consider that aren't necessarily about ingredients or recipe specifics. Here is an overview of the most common issues.

TRANSPORTING FOOD

Every recipe in this book takes into consideration that the dish will probably have to be transported, and most of the recipes include advice on how to do that. But there are a few things that are important to keep in mind always:

- If you fully cook your dish and then dash out the door, hoping to deliver it still hot, keep in mind that it will continue cooking from that residual heat. If you then pop it in a warm oven upon arriving, it could quickly go from perfect to sad and overcooked. Often the better option is to parcook it and then let the dish cool down, reheating it once you arrive. If you are going to keep your dish warm for a prolonged period, just make sure you've factored that in as a bit of extra cooking time.

- Always make sure you have everything tightly covered, even if you're not going far. A sudden turn in a car or a slosh from a misstep can quickly turn into a disaster. The more tightly sealed your containers, the better they will move.

- You don't have to invest in bags that keep dishes hot or cold, but they can really work wonders. If you are toting dishes to meals frequently, an insulated bag may be a valuable investment.

STORING FOOD

Keeping your food safe for a day or two is just as important as how you move it.

- For many hot dishes, it's best to let them fully cool down before you refrigerate them. You can heat up your fridge (and all of its contents) if you put a piping hot pot inside. You also don't want food to keep cooking: once you cover a hot dish tightly it will keep cooking from the stored heat (I can't emphasize this enough). So if you are storing a dish, let it cool down without a top before covering it and putting it in the fridge. For anything in a pot or saucepan, you can set it in a sink of ice water, halfway up the sides, to cool it quickly. (This could be risky with a baking dish if it's not very deep!)

- You don't need to have the perfect container to store food effectively. If you want to store something well, I learned a trick from acclaimed chef Michael White: first cover the dish with a layer of plastic wrap, tape it down, and then add aluminum foil on top. Just be sure, again, that the dish has cooled down completely.

BAKING DISH SIZES

——◆——

One of my least favorite parts of cookbooks is the insistence on specific baking dish sizes. I imagine most people have a collection of dishes, but no one has everything. Sometimes during a marathon cooking session, the specific pan a recipe calls for is already in use. If I'm lacking the exact size pan the recipe calls for, I usually start to panic, concerned that everything will fall apart. In this book you won't find many pan dimensions because many of the recipes are flexible. Some are more wedded to a particular size dish—pies are usually best in a pie pan, for example—but for the most part, see if what you have will accommodate the food. The recipes in this book will work fine in dishes of a few different sizes, as long as the pot or dish is generally large enough, so don't sweat it if you don't have an endless array of cookware. I know this might drive some people nuts, but the goal is freedom from casserole-dish tyranny.

BE MINDFUL OF FOOD SITTING OUT

——◆——

This is the part where I tell you to be careful about food safety, so I apologize for the lecture. But I really don't want anyone to think that my recipes got them sick after leaving a dish out in the sun. So let me say this: if you wouldn't leave your milk or meat sitting out on the counter for 6 hours, don't leave your

dinner sitting out. Use common sense. I like the idea of leaving dishes out for an open-ended meal—my favorite picnics are the ones where we sit and graze for hours—but if something would be better refrigerated then be mindful. It's always important to plan ahead and make sure you have thought through the timing. You can always bring a few frozen ice packs and tuck them under your dish to keep it cool.

OVENS

——◆——

Let's talk about that fickle friend the oven. Like people, every oven is different. They all have hot and cold spots, and too much action can make them misbehave. Every recipe in this book has been tested alone, with only one dish in the oven at a time. This means that if you are cooking multiple things at once, they may not all cook evenly or exactly as described. The timing on recipes is flexible for a reason: check on all your dishes as they are cooking and shuffle them around the oven to avoid hot spots or overcooking as needed. (This is a good tip for any large meal, like Thanksgiving, when all appliances are used to the max.)

On a different oven note, never assume there is oven space at the temperature you need if you are going to a party. Several people may be bringing dishes to warm, and the host's single oven may soon become crowded. So ask ahead if you are bringing a dish that needs heat.

REHEATING

———•———

Be careful with reheating: low and slow is usually the best mode of operating. If your dish is going from refrigerator to oven, it's good to leave it out for half an hour or so to come to room temperature before reheating. That way you're not adding too much extra heat to get it up to temperature. Every recipe is different, but the one constant is to take your time and plan ahead.

HEAT NAMES

———•———

What exactly *is* medium-high heat? A lot of cooking terminology is completely subjective: you'll need to get to know your stove to be familiar with the settings. Most people don't have thermometers at home, so I have tried to avoid getting too technical here. But it is important to keep in mind that if the heat is high, that probably means you need your hood or fan on: don't be afraid of high heat. On the other side, make sure to look at the visual cues in every recipe and not just the timing or heat level. If the onions cook for 5 minutes, or until translucent, give them enough time to cook to doneness rather than pulling them off the heat after exactly 5 minutes. Always take into consideration the description in tandem with the cooking times.

recipe notes to consider

Every cook has his or her own conventions, so let's make sure we are all on the same page.

SERVING SIZES

—•—

I've made serving sizes here as though each dish is a big part of a meal for six to eight people. If you are having a ton of people bringing a ton of dishes, you don't necessarily need to size up as much as you think: keep in mind that the more dishes available, the smaller the portions people will take from each. Then again, the dishes in this book will hopefully inspire seconds or thirds. You *can* also scale anything up as needed: every dish in this book, unless indicated, can easily be doubled or tripled if needed for a large crowd. As long as everything stays in proportion, you should be good to go.

EXACT MEASUREMENTS AND SUBSTITUTIONS

—•—

The hardest part for me about writing a book is that I am a substituter and a poor measurer. I like to taste and throw in an extra half a lemon or another pinch of salt. And I imagine many of you are the same way. I actually encourage that: Don't have leeks? That's okay. Use the onion you have lying in your produce drawer. Don't want to buy an entire jar of allspice for one recipe? Substitute that with cinnamon bought for something else. These recipes work well as written, but they aren't dogmatic. Even the baking recipes intentionally contain a little wiggle room; this is not the kind of cooking that requires a scale. I want it to be easy and relaxing to cook from *Bring It!*, which is why so many recipes take 30 minutes or less to prepare. If you aren't a confident cook then by all means, keep it exact. But don't be afraid to use what you have either: this book is supposed to make your life easier, not harder. The most important thing to keep in mind is the ratios. If you are making a tart, for example, don't add an extra half a cup of an ingredient or the filling might not fit into the shell. Keep the proportions in mind, and if you're like me, your substitutions should work fine.

BRINING

—•—

The extra step of brining (submerging meat in a salt bath for a few hours, or rubbing salt and spices on meat a few hours ahead) has become one of the most contentious things in cooking. I have glazed over during many Thanksgiving conversations where people insist that their turkey brine—the wet brine! the dry brine! the cider brine! the special secret ingredient brine!—has changed their life. You certainly don't have to, but some of the recipes in this book include an extra step to brine. And I'll take it further and say you could do it for almost any meat. Especially for recipes where you are often serving proteins cold or reheating them, having a bit of extra moisture definitely does not hurt. If you have some extra time, strongly consider it.

a few notes on ingredients

SALT: When salt is an ingredient, kosher or freshly ground sea salt are implied. I rarely give you the satisfaction of an exact measurement. It's usually just described as "salt to taste." Why? Because it's so personal. Everyone has a different salt preference. Unless a dish cannot be tasted midway through (like a quiche or a raw meat marinade), I think it's best to taste as you go. You can always add more, but you can't subtract, so be gentle with your salt. "To taste" can mean any amount that makes sense to you: keep adding until it feels right.

EGGS: Eggs in recipes are always large and fresh. If you want to save money, feel free to choose eggs that work for you. But if you can splurge a bit, I think there is a difference to be had in antibiotic-free and cage-free eggs, and if you can get them from a farmers' market (lucky you!), that's even better. If you want to buy premium eggs only when necessary, use them for dishes in which eggs are the star. You'll notice your delicious fresh eggs much more in deviled eggs or egg salad than you would in chocolate cookies.

HERBS: When I mention herbs, I always mean fresh herbs, unless it is specifically noted. Fresh herbs bring food to life and aren't necessarily interchangeable with dried herbs. That said, if you have to substitute, it'll mostly be okay, especially in cooked dishes. (I wouldn't suggest substituting dried herbs for fresh in a salad or puréed sauce.) Just keep in mind that some dried herbs are stronger than others, so you'll want to taste and gradually add small amounts so that you don't put too much in. Generally, approximately 1 teaspoon of dried herbs is equivalent to 1 tablespoon of fresh herbs.

GARLIC CLOVES: I like to use fresh garlic, and when a clove is asked for I mean a medium to large one. If you have a head of garlic that has small cloves, you can always use two in place of the one large one. Garlic is also a bit like salt: it's dependent on your preference, so don't be afraid to use a little less or more if you have strong feelings. On a similar note, while I think fresh garlic is better, I am also not immune to the ease of preminced garlic. If you're going that route then use 1½ teaspoons of preminced garlic for each clove.

OLIVE OIL: Always use extra-virgin olive oil. There's no excuse not to.

LEMONS: There are few things I feel more strongly about than using fresh lemon juice rather than bottled. While preminced garlic or dried herbs might be acceptable substitutes in a pinch, I will never believe that lemon juice can be from anything but a fresh lemon. The taste just does not compare. So please try to keep it fresh. Using fresh lemon in a recipe isn't an exact science. You'll see a lot of recipes that call for "the juice of 1 lemon," but lemon sizes vary widely. I find that if you squeeze a lemon and measure the juice, you'll always have some left over, so unless the exact measurement is especially important for a particular recipe, use whatever amount of juice you can get from your lemon and add more to taste. If you have small lemons, you can always squeeze another half and taste as you go.

PIE CRUSTS: My grandmother used to make the greatest pie crusts. She was very old school: she used lard and avoided touching the ingredients too much with her hands so heat was never transferred to the dough. She took pie making seriously, and the result was a perfect flaky pie crust every time. It made even the simplest pie taste incredible. That being said, I am not a pie crust snob. In fact in my own home, I am happy to admit that I rarely take the time to do it. Store-bought pie crusts won't get you that flaky lightness, but they will get the job done. So choose whichever version you want. I've included my grandmother's pie crust recipe here if you want to take the time—but if not, it'll all be okay.

a word about precut ingredients and shortcuts

Life is short, and we are all too busy to be judgmental about whatever shortcuts make our lives easier. I once did an interview with a well-known television chef who derided precut ingredients and people who didn't make their own butter. As a mom and a full-time journalist, there are many days I want to cook but do not have the energy to break down an entire butternut squash. So on those days, I am perfectly content to buy the fresh precut version. Preminced garlic or a store-bought pie crust might actually be the thing that saves you from heating up a jar of tomato sauce for dinner. Don't sweat the small stuff. It will be delicious. Do whatever you need to do to find joy in the kitchen, and the rest will fall into place.

how to use this book

The recipes are divided up into six different chapters: Hors d'Oeuvres and Dips; Salads; Casseroles, Pasta, and Tarts; Meats and Fish; Veggies and Grains; and Desserts. But there are three other distinctions that might help you choose what to make. Each recipe sports badges like "Fridge to Table," "Day Ahead," and "30 Minutes or Less." When thinking of a dish to bring, these are often the three categories that must be considered.

a few points on the badges

"**FRIDGE TO TABLE**" also includes room temperature and doesn't mean the dish *has* to be served cold. Some of the recipes with this badge indicate recipes that could go either hot or cold: it just gives you the option.

Similarly, "**DAY AHEAD**" doesn't mean the dish *has* to be made a day ahead. It's just a sign that this is a dish you can make on your own schedule, and it will hold nicely overnight.

Keep in mind that "**30 MINUTES OR LESS**" is an estimate: if I asked my husband to prep the ingredients, then some of these recipes could take over an hour (sorry babe, but it's true). There's no right or wrong speed, but this note is just an indication that these recipes are on the quicker side.

The main goal here is to keep it easy and fun. These are all recipes I have made for my friends and family around my dinner table or brought over to their houses. I make them for Christmas dinners, Super Bowl parties, and picnics in the park. Every Thursday night for a year I made these recipes diligently and then let my siblings have at them: they critiqued them to no end, and the ones they didn't love didn't make it into this book. These recipes were then tested in kitchens across America by dedicated friends who tweaked them again and again to near perfection. This is all to say that this book was made with love for the home cooks who don't have the time or energy for recipe failure. I know what it's like to have people over for dinner and want to impress them. I know what it's like to bring food for a new baby or for someone who is ill and want to be sure that I am bringing food that will make them feel cherished. Don't be afraid to *Bring It!*: these recipes were made for it.

22

CHAPTER 2

Hors d'Oeuvres and Dips

Before any meal turns serious, a few snacks
always need to be on hand. The key to a great
hors d'oeuvre or dip at a shared gathering is similar
to the main meal: it needs to be universal, travel
well, and most importantly eaten with ease before
everyone starts piling onto their dinner plates.
If you've volunteered for the premeal nosh,
you're up first, so try and keep it as simple
as possible on arrival.

hors d'oeuvres and dips

RECIPES

Deviled Eggs with Shrimp

It's pretty hard to go wrong with a deviled egg. They are easy to make, beautiful to look at, and simple to eat. You can always spot a few people standing in a corner, wondering how many eggs they have consumed before the meal has even begun. And for group meals they are particularly great because they don't take up precious oven space.

This version is based on a dear family friend's recipe. Louise was renowned for her deviled eggs, and I never had a holiday without them. She had two secret ingredients. The first is a deviled egg throwback that often gets sidelined in these more artisanal times: pickle relish. A little tangy, a little sweet, and easy to procure, it is a classic for a reason. But the second ingredient is a bit more nontraditional. She always used sweet local shrimp from her "shrimp guy." You might not have your own personal shrimp guy, but using any shrimp will add a texture and depth that will change your deviled egg status quo forever.

MAKES 12 DEVILED EGGS

1 tablespoon extra-virgin olive oil

6 small uncooked shrimp (or 3 large), peeled and deveined

Salt to taste

6 eggs

3 tablespoons mayonnaise

1 tablespoon pickle relish

1 teaspoon brown mustard

Paprika, for garnish

Bring a pot of water to a boil. Set aside ice water in a large bowl, deep enough to submerge the 6 eggs.

In a small skillet, heat the olive oil over medium heat and sauté the shrimp until just cooked. Salt to taste, remove from the heat, then cool completely and finely dice.

When the water is boiling, boil the eggs (preferably slightly older eggs so they are easier to peel) for 10 to 12 minutes depending on size: extra-large eggs need closer to 12 minutes, and medium to large eggs only take 10. They should be just hardboiled, ideally with the very center of the yolk still a bit soft.

(recipe continues)

When they are done, submerge them in the ice water bath. Alternatively, you can run cold water over them for 5 minutes.

Peel the eggs and cut them in half, removing the yolks from the whites. Lightly smash the yolks with a fork until they are roughly blended together and then measure them. Whatever the amount of yolk, add three-quarters that amount of mayonnaise to the yolks (roughly 3 tablespoons), and then mix together. Be careful not to blend too smooth, as the texture is important. Add the fully cooled shrimp, pickle relish, brown mustard, and a generous dash of salt to the bowl. Mix all ingredients well. Add to a piping bag (or a zip-top bag with a small hole cut in the corner to resemble a piping bag) and pipe the yolk into the centers of the whites. Top with paprika and serve.

— SUBSTITUTIONS —

There are endless substitutions for deviled eggs and sometimes that can be half the fun. You can easily take the shrimp out if you are vegetarian—although it really is the best secret ingredient, so don't eliminate it unless you have to. And if you do, try to add something else—small diced cucumber or carrots—for texture. Or you can double down and add an extra shrimp on top for decoration. You can always add color to your deviled eggs by adding beets or blended greens or carrots to the mixture. And some people will always love more mustard—these are preferences and they are easy to adjust. You can also add great toppings to your eggs instead of the paprika—a piece of bacon, salmon roe, pickles, olives, dill, smoked salmon. Almost anything works, and that is the beauty of the recipe. It is great as is but can always be adjusted to taste.

— HOW TO BRING IT —

Deviled eggs can be made up to 2 days ahead and refrigerated but make sure to add the paprika at the very end, otherwise it will dissolve into the yolk. Press plastic wrap (very) gently into the yolks if you've fully assembled the eggs ahead of time, and be careful to transport them carefully so they don't tip. You can always reshape the tops a bit with the spoon if you need to: the paprika will cover a lot of imperfections. You can also assemble the dish on arrival, bringing the yolk filling in the plastic bag and egg whites separately. Just make sure to ask in advance if you can claim a bit of counter space to finish the eggs. You can serve them cold or at room temperature.

Pear and Blue Cheese Endive Boats

I am such a sucker for appetizers that are self-contained. But I'm also pretty tired of seeing the same old mousses and cheeses on top of a cracker. This appetizer has a formal look but is simple and has a fresh, rich flavor. The boats would be a great choice for an hors d'oeuvre passed around at a party.

**MAKES ABOUT 20 BOATS
(6 TO 8 SERVINGS)**

2 ripe pears, cored and diced (about 3 cups)

2 teaspoons balsamic vinegar

3 teaspoons fresh lemon juice

1⅓ cups (8 to 10 ounces) crumbled blue cheese

Salt to taste

3 to 4 heads of endive, separated into individual leaves

2 tablespoons finely chopped mint, for garnish

Combine the pears, vinegar, lemon juice, cheese, and salt in a bowl. Carefully stir until incorporated. Line up the endive leaves with the cup facing up. Spoon the pear and blue cheese mixture into each leaf. Sprinkle the chopped mint over the top.

NOTE: This is a taste-as-you-go recipe. The strength of the blue cheese can determine the quantity you need. The ratios here were made using a fairly mild, precrumbled blue cheese. So if you are using a stronger blue cheese, you may want to adjust down the amount accordingly.

— HOW TO BRING IT —

If you're traveling far you may want to do the last phase of spooning out on arrival: you don't want your little boats to tip over. The boats will last in the fridge for up to 12 hours if you've completed them; just make sure to cover with plastic wrap or aluminum foil. You can store the ingredients for 24 hours if you store the filling and endive separately.

Stuffed Mushrooms

The phrase "stuffed mushrooms" often brings to mind a flavorless vegetarian dish at a party, but this recipe turns that convention on its head. The deep flavor of roasted mushrooms is a perfect pair for sausage, and in this recipe these two flavors blend together into a simple, delightful little finger food. One thing to keep in mind: the size of the mushrooms doesn't matter in execution but it does change the amount of stuffing. If your mushrooms are larger, you can always increase the amount of the filling.

MAKES 12 MUSHROOMS

½ cup fresh sausage (about 1 sausage link, casing removed)

2 garlic cloves, diced

½ cup (4 ounces) goat cheese

2 teaspoons fresh thyme

½ teaspoon soy sauce

½ teaspoon salt (or to taste)

12 button mushrooms, at least 2 inches across, stems removed

1 tablespoon extra-virgin olive oil

Preheat the oven to 350°F.

Set a skillet over medium heat and cook the sausage and garlic for approximately 5 minutes, until the sausage starts to brown. Crumble it into small pieces so it can stuff more easily into the mushrooms. Combine the sausage mixture with the goat cheese, thyme, soy sauce, and salt. Rub the outsides of the mushrooms with olive oil. Spoon the stuffing into the mushrooms. Bake for 25 minutes. They can be served hot or at room temperature.

NOTE: Also keep in mind that you will have leftover mushroom stems: you can always sauté them and add them into the stuffing if you'd like, or keep them for an omelet the next day.

— HOW TO BRING IT —

These actually store well for up to 3 days well wrapped and refrigerated; just be sure to bring them to at least room temperature before serving. You can place them in a 350°F oven for 5 to 10 minutes to get them a bit warm if you'd like: they hold up well and aren't in as much danger of overcooking like some other dishes. But if you're planning on eating them at room temperature anyway, skip the reheating entirely.

Ham and Eggplant Toast

Eggplant can be divisive: some people don't like the tough skin or bitter seeds. But this recipe removes all the conflict and just offers up the best part—its creamy interior. It's a nod to baba ghanoush, the Middle Eastern charred eggplant dip, but with a ham-infused twist. There are a few important caveats: use the smaller Italian eggplants if you can find them. The larger the eggplant, the more seeds it will have and the more bitter the flavor. And try to buy a high-quality ham. The better your ingredients are, the better this dish will be.

MAKES 24 SMALL TOASTS

2 medium size or 3 small eggplants

1 garlic clove, very finely chopped or grated

1 tablespoon fresh lemon juice

1/4 teaspoon ground cumin

1/2 teaspoon grated lemon zest

Dash of salt

6 slices multigrain bread

4 ounces thinly sliced ham or prosciutto

1 teaspoon finely diced chives

Turn on the broiler. Line a sheet pan with aluminum foil and place the eggplants on top. Put the eggplants under the broiler, at least 4 inches away from the heat source.

Cook for 30 minutes, turning occasionally, until the eggplants are completely charred on all sides and very tender (if you are using one large eggplant, cook for at least 45 minutes).

Remove from the oven and wrap the foil from the pan around the eggplants. Let them rest for at least 20 minutes. Once the eggplants have cooled, remove the foil and slice them in half. Scoop out the soft interior and place in a bowl; add the garlic, lemon, cumin, lemon zest, and salt and mix well.

Cut the bread into quarters and spread the eggplant mixture on top of the bread. Cut the ham into slices to fit the bread quarters and place on top. Sprinkle the chives (and a bit more salt if you'd like) on top.

— HOW TO BRING IT —

The eggplant part of this dish can be made up to 2 days ahead and stored in the refrigerator. But try not to plate it until an hour or so before serving: there is nothing worse than stale bread that once was fresh. If you can plate on arrival, that is ideal; otherwise, make sure to cover it tightly so the bread stays as fresh as possible.

Fig, Goat Cheese, and Rosemary Toast

This recipe is from my mother-in-law. She served it as part of a spread for brunch, and it instantly livens up any table. When I first tasted it, I immediately said, "Oh, I need to have that one in my repertoire." The flavors come together in perfect harmony in this simple-to-make dish. Keep this recipe in your back pocket for that day when there's not much time to make a great starter. It is so much more than the sum of its parts.

MAKES 20 SMALL TOASTS

8 to 10 fresh figs (about 1 cup when sliced)

5 slices whole wheat bread (preferably a high-quality bakery loaf)

4 ounces soft goat cheese

1 tablespoon very finely chopped rosemary

Drizzle of honey

Dash of salt

Slice the figs into discs about ½ inch thick. Cut each slice of bread into 4 triangles. Spread the goat cheese on the bread. Lay the fig slices on top of the goat cheese and then sprinkle the rosemary on top. Drizzle the honey evenly across the toast (it should be a very small amount since the figs are already sweet) and then finish with the salt.

— HOW TO BRING IT —

This dish is sturdy enough to travel, but the bread needs to stay fresh: you don't want to make it a day in advance or even more than a few hours ahead. Luckily it is so quick and easy you won't need to. Just make sure to tightly cover it with aluminum foil until the moment you are serving.

— SUBSTITUTIONS —

This dish works best with fresh figs in season, but in a pinch you could use the dried variety; just keep in mind that it won't taste quite as summer fresh. If you do use dried figs, which are fairly sweet and concentrated, eliminate the honey and reduce the amount of figs by half. You could also substitute apples or pears for the figs for a slightly different take on the same idea.

Prosciutto-Wrapped Asparagus

This recipe is a classic party hors d'oeuvre taken to a whole new level. The prosciutto and asparagus are delicious on their own, but the lemon, butter, and yolk dressing add an umami perfection. It will surprise people who don't expect to have that extra flavor hidden inside. This is the perfect little start to a meal or it can even work as a side dish. Just be prepared for them to disappear quickly.

MAKES 6 TO 8 SERVINGS

4 tablespoons unsalted butter

1 pound asparagus, trimmed

Salt and freshly ground black pepper to taste

2 tablespoons fresh lemon juice (about ½ a lemon)

2 egg yolks, beaten

8 ounces prosciutto or other thinly sliced ham

Put the butter in a wide skillet over medium-high heat. Add ¼ cup of water and bring to a simmer. Place the asparagus in the skillet (the asparagus should fit in a single layer) and cover. Cook for 3 minutes or until the asparagus is cooked but still firm and bright green.

Remove the asparagus from the skillet and set aside, sprinkling with salt.

Add the lemon juice, salt, and pepper to the skillet. Cook and stir for 2 minutes until the mixture has thickened.

Remove from the heat and pour the liquid into a bowl with the egg yolks. Quickly whip the egg yolks with the butter mixture until it has all incorporated. Be careful to do this step fast: you don't want the yolks to cook before you can start whisking.

Spread the sauce on one side of each piece of prosciutto. Make sure not to spread it too thick: a thin but purposeful layer will do. Wrap the asparagus in the prosciutto so that the prosciutto covers almost all of the asparagus stalks, with the sauce on the inside. Place on a platter and serve.

— HOW TO BRING IT —

These can be made up to 2 days ahead and refrigerated as long as they are tightly covered.

Baked Feta

Cheese is often relegated to a topping or one component of a plate of appetizers. Rarely does it get to be the headlining star of the dish. But when you bake feta something magical happens, and it deserves to stand on its own. This dish is simpler than other baked feta recipes that overwhelm by adding in olives and tomatoes. This recipe keeps the focus on the feta with a few extra touches: the spice of the chili flakes, the boldness of the herbs and lemon, the texture of the nuts. And that also means you can serve it with crackers or even eat it unaccompanied. It's one of those appetizers you can throw together quickly but doesn't feel rushed. It works great as an appetizer, or you can double (triple? quadruple?) the recipe for a larger party.

MAKES 4 SERVINGS

1 block (8 to 10 ounces) feta

2 tablespoons fresh lemon juice (about ½ a lemon)

¼ teaspoon red chili flakes

1 tablespoon chopped parsley

1 tablespoon chopped basil

2 tablespoons walnuts, chopped

Preheat the oven to 350°F. Place the feta in a small baking dish: if your feta is in a square block, you can cut it in half to fill more of the dish. Sprinkle the lemon juice, chili flakes, parsley, basil, and walnuts on top. Place in the oven and bake 10 to 12 minutes, or until the feta starts to just appear melty. Serve hot.

— HOW TO BRING IT —

This dish, which takes very little time to make, can be prepped ahead of time. Since the time in the oven is so quick, just throw it in the oven on arrival. If you're at an event where the oven temperature is set a little bit above or below, that's fine: this is a pretty forgiving dish that will come out well, as long as the oven isn't *too* hot.

Fancy Egg Salad

Just saying "egg salad" can make some people snooze. Yet there's a reason the idea has stuck around so long. Eggs are glorious and can go well beyond breakfast food. But how do you make a staple of lunch boxes feel like an exciting dish to bring along? In this recipe we have two tricks. The first is tarragon, an herb more common in French recipes but one whose distinctive flavor is often underused elsewhere. Here it marries perfectly with the eggs. The second is salmon roe. I know this is a slightly higher-end ingredient, but since the rest of the dish is so accessible, it is one worth having. It not only adds a briny pop to the flavor, but layered on top it creates a pretty visual that is hard to resist—roe is a less expensive cousin to caviar, often used in sushi rolls. And roe are eggs, so it all fits together.

MAKES 4 TO 6 SERVINGS

8 large eggs

½ cup mayonnaise

1 tablespoon finely chopped tarragon, plus leaves for garnish

2 teaspoons white wine vinegar or apple cider vinegar

Salt and freshly ground black pepper to taste

4 ounces salmon roe

Bring a large pot of water to a boil. Set aside ice water in a large bowl, deep enough to submerge the 8 eggs. When the water comes to a boil, lower the eggs in carefully with a spoon and cook for 10 minutes. Drain the water and place the eggs in the ice water bath for at least 5 minutes.

Peel the eggs and then roughly chop them. Stir the eggs together with the mayonnaise, tarragon, vinegar, salt, and pepper. Taste after combining the ingredients to make sure you have enough salt and pepper. Place the eggs in a shallow bowl and spread the roe on top as thinly as you can so that most of the top is covered. Garnish with an extra tarragon leaf or two. Serve with crackers or bread.

— SUBSTITUTIONS —

This recipe works well with any fish eggs, so use whatever your grocery store or fishmonger has. Whitefish roe, trout roe, or even caviar (if you are really looking to splurge and impress) will work great here. If you are using a very shallow bowl, you can use another 2 ounces of salmon roe, but don't go beyond that: too much roe will overpower the egg salad quickly.

— HOW TO BRING IT —

You can make this a day ahead; just be sure to cover tightly so the roe doesn't dry out. You may even want to put an extra layer of plastic wrap delicately on top of the roe to keep them fresh.

Perfect Baked Wings

These wings are as crispy as you can get without a fryer. I make them every year for the Super Bowl, and at this point I think I have some friends who only keep me around so they can have their annual wing fix. They are, however, slightly more logistically challenging than other recipes in this book. You can prep everything ahead and make the sauce, but you need to plan ahead. That being said: it's worth it. Leaving the uncooked chicken wings in the refrigerator overnight dries the skin, making the wings extra crispy later, when you bake them. Although wings are best served hot, the crispy skin performs even if served at room temperature. Crispy wings with a tangy sauce are a combination no one can resist.

**MAKES ABOUT 40 WINGS
(6 TO 10 SERVINGS)**

FOR THE WINGS

4 pounds chicken wings

1 tablespoon baking powder

1 tablespoon salt

½ teaspoon freshly ground black pepper

FOR THE SAUCE

4 tablespoons salted butter, melted

¼ teaspoon cayenne pepper

¼ cup hot sauce (Frank's RedHot preferred)

Make sure your wings are cut into drumettes and flats with the tips removed. They typically come this way, but if not, make sure to use a sharp knife to cut them into half so that you have wings and drums separated. Pat wings dry with paper towels to remove any moisture. Stir the baking powder, salt, and pepper together and rub thoroughly and evenly into the wings. Cover a sheet pan with aluminum foil and place the wings evenly on the tray. Refrigerate for 10 to 24 hours (the range is very flexible). Turn the wings over halfway through, or you can also place the wings on a wire rack and skip the turning step.

Preheat the oven to 400°F.

To make the sauce, mix together the butter, pepper, and hot sauce in a large bowl. Bake the wings for 20 minutes, turn them over, then cook an additional 20 minutes. Depending on how crisp you'd like them, you can cook for an additional 5 to 10 minutes, watching carefully and flipping as needed to get the wings crisped up. Add the wings to the bowl with the sauce, and toss to coat thoroughly.

NOTE: These wings are only a tiny bit spicy. If you like them spicier, you can always add more cayenne; just make sure all of your guests are on board.

— SUBSTITUTIONS —

You can easily substitute this particular sauce for other wing sauces you like. Ginger and soy sauce combine for a great one. Melted salted butter with a bit of garlic powder is also tasty.

— HOW TO BRING IT —

This dish is all about the timing: it is great for an event because all of the components can be made ahead. The sauce can be stored for up to a week in the refrigerator and quickly reheated in the microwave to get it back to the right consistency. And the wings already sit for hours before cooking, so they can just be popped into the oven when everyone is ready.

If you want to fully cook them beforehand, it's fine to serve them hot or at room temperature: bake them and let them cool, then refrigerate for up to a day on wire racks covered in aluminum foil. Remove them from the fridge at least 30 minutes before you want to serve them to let them come to room temperature, then coat them in the sauce before serving. If you want to serve them hot, slightly underbake them the first time by reducing the cooking time by 5 to 10 minutes and then crisp them in the oven for 5 to 10 minutes, turning once, just before serving. Either way, hot or cold, only add the sauce right before serving: the crispy skin will stay crisp as long as they cool properly before storing, are stored in a single layer, and aren't sauced until right before serving.

Flavored Popcorn

Few snacks are greater than popped corn, but why do we get stuck in the rut of butter, cheese, or caramel? There are so many other flavor options that aren't as time consuming to make as caramel or as sticky as cheesy powder. Following are a few options with the same basic principles: use microwave popcorn in a bag so that you don't have to worry about the stovetop; add flavorings that stick on once you give the bag a good shake so there's no mess; and use easy-to find ingredients. It's a delicious starter, game-day snack, or even a bagged gift. Each of these flavors makes enough to season one standard-size bag of microwave popcorn.

Spicy Smoked Paprika Popcorn

1 teaspoon smoked paprika

1 teaspoon garlic powder

1 teaspoon fine salt

1 tablespoon melted butter

Combine the paprika, garlic powder, and salt in one bowl, and the melted butter in another. Continue with directions on the next page.

Orange and Vanilla Popcorn

3 tablespoons grated orange zest

2 teaspoons granulated sugar

½ teaspoon vanilla extract

1 tablespoon melted butter

Combine the zest and sugar in one small bowl and the vanilla extract and melted butter in another. Continue with directions on the next page.

Chocolate Popcorn

2 teaspoons cocoa powder

2 teaspoons granulated sugar

½ teaspoon cinnamon

1 teaspoon melted butter

Combine the cocoa powder, sugar, and cinnamon together in one bowl with the melted butter in another bowl. Continue with directions on the next page.

Lemon Lime Popcorn

1 tablespoon grated lemon zest

1 tablespoon grated lime zest

2 teaspoons minced fresh cilantro

1 teaspoon fine salt

Combine all ingredients together in a bowl and continue with directions on the next page.

Pizza Popcorn

3 tablespoons very finely grated Parmesan cheese

2 teaspoons dried basil

½ teaspoon garlic powder

½ teaspoon fine salt

2 teaspoons tomato paste

2 tablespoons melted butter

Combine the cheese, basil, garlic powder, and salt in one small bowl. Add the tomato paste to the butter and fully combine (a fork or small whisk is best). Continue with directions below.

ADDITIONAL INGREDIENTS

1 (3.5 ounce) bag of good-quality microwave popcorn. Try to find the plainest version with no extra flavoring: if it includes butter or salt, you may need to adjust butter and salt amounts in the recipes.

1 paper lunch bag

With all the ingredients set out per the previous instructions, pop the popcorn according to the instructions on the bag.

When it is finished quickly pour half of the popcorn in the paper bag and then pour half of your chosen flavoring ingredients into both bags: the goal here is to move fast enough that the popcorn is still hot and to evenly distribute the toppings on the popcorn. Fold both bags tightly to close, and with one in each hand shake the bags. There should be plenty of room in both bags to really shake that popcorn. Pour the popcorn into serving bowls.

— SUBSTITUTIONS —

You can use stovetop popcorn here, of course. I use microwave bags in this recipe because it's easier, but feel free to use whatever version makes sense for you. If you do use the stovetop, make the popcorn in a pot and then place the lid back on to shake the pot and distribute the seasonings on the popcorn.

— HOW TO BRING IT —

If you have access to a microwave at the place where your meal is held, it's easy enough to make right beforehand. Bring the toppings in separate containers, and microwave the butter and the popcorn on arrival. But if you can't make them on-site, then all of these popcorn flavors can be made up to 24 hours ahead if you store them in an airtight container.

Guacamole Three Ways

Guacamole has now become such a staple that you may feel like you can never have enough on hand. For a new spin, here are three different flavors: a favorite basic version, a slightly sweeter version with oranges, and a nuttier version with a bit of texture. Contrary to what you might think, you can absolutely make it in advance with little to no browning! Cover it tightly then stir on arrival, and you shouldn't have a problem.

**MAKES ABOUT 6 CUPS
(10 TO 15 SERVINGS)**

15 ripe avocados

Juice of 6 limes

2 large ripe tomatoes, seeded and diced, divided

2 jalapeño peppers, seeded and finely diced, divided

1/2 cup finely diced red onion, divided

3 tablespoons chopped cilantro

Salt to taste

1 orange, peeled and diced (preferably blood orange if in season)

3 tablespoons fresh, chopped mint

1/4 cup pistachios

1/4 cup almonds

1/4 cup diced radishes
(1 to 3, depending on size)

Cut each avocado in half, remove the pit, and then dice. (I recommend making cuts in the flesh lengthwise and crosswise so that the avocado is in small cubes, and then using a spoon to remove it from the peel.) Add the lime juice and combine. Divide evenly into three bowls.

For basic guacamole: To one bowl of avocado, add half the tomatoes, half the jalapeños, half the onion, the cilantro, and salt to taste. Stir well to combine.

For orange guacamole: To a second bowl of avocado, add the orange, mint, and the remaining red onion and jalapeño. Add salt to taste and stir well to combine.

For nut guacamole: Put the pistachios and almonds in the blender and pulse until the nuts are in pieces (but not too fine). Add to the remaining bowl of avocado with the radishes, remaining tomato, and salt to taste.

Sample each guacamole individually because the amount of salt is truly to taste here.

Serve cold with tortilla chips within 6 hours of making the guacamole or it will begin to brown. If it browns a bit, stir before putting it out.

— HOW TO BRING IT —

Air will oxidize the avocado, causing it to brown, so although it travels easily, you should only make it 6 hours ahead at most. If you aren't serving the guacamole immediately, you can add a bit of extra lime juice on top and then cover it tightly with plastic wrap, pressing it down onto the surface. For another method for preventing oxidation, add a thin layer of water on top before covering it in plastic wrap; pour off the water when you are ready to serve. The water keeps the guacamole fresher, but it's a little harder to transport. Either way works fine, depending on what seems easiest to you. Keeping the guacamole refrigerated until the last minute will also help.

Salmon Cucumbers

There are few dishes that look as fancy with as little work as salmon cucumbers. The color of the salmon against the backdrop of the cucumber makes for a perfect little bite. This dish can be prepared ahead and travels well, and since the cucumber slices make individual bites, they are great for passing around at a party.

MAKES 15 TO 20 CUCUMBER BITES

1 tablespoon extra-virgin olive oil

2 tablespoons diced shallots

½ pound salmon fillet

1 large English cucumber

Salt to taste

¼ cup mayonnaise

¼ teaspoon hot sauce (Frank's RedHot preferred)

2 tablespoons capers

3 tablespoons chopped chives, for garnish

Freshly ground black pepper to taste

Place a pan on medium-high heat. Add the olive oil and shallots and sauté for 3 minutes. Move the shallots to one side of the pan and then add the salmon and sauté for 4 minutes. Flip and cook an additional 2 to 4 minutes, depending on the thickness of your salmon and how rare you like it. Remove from heat and let cool.

Slice the cucumber into disks, approximately ¼ inch thick: they should be thick enough to hold the filling on top but not so thick that they will take over. In a bowl combine the salt, mayonnaise, hot sauce, and capers. Flake the salmon into small pieces and add into the bowl. Mix until combined. Spoon the salmon mixture on top of the cucumbers, and top with chives and freshly ground pepper.

— HOW TO BRING IT —

This dish can be made a day in advance as long as it is covered well in plastic wrap: you don't want the salmon or cucumber to dry out. You can place the cucumbers on a serving platter and refrigerate, or you can put them on a sheet pan and then transfer them when you are ready to serve. Just don't stack them or the cucumbers will get soggy.

Alternatively, if you would rather assemble on arrival, you can certainly do that as well. Just make sure you have the time and space to do it wherever you are going.

Pimento Cheese and Crab Dip

Pimento cheese is like a religion in some parts of the country. It can be used in everything from dips to sandwiches, served hot or cold, and eaten morning, noon, and night. My take adds a bit more decadence to the proceedings without a lot of extra work by throwing in some crab. It is topped with panko crumbs (Japanese breadcrumbs), which give it a little bit of extra texture. But this Southern recipe is also the best kind of dish for a gathering: easy to make, full of flavor, and travels well. It can be served bubbling hot or at room temperature depending on the setting.

MAKES 8 TO 10 SERVINGS

1 pound sharp Cheddar cheese, grated

1 (7-ounce) jar pimentos, drained

1½ tablespoons Worcestershire sauce

2 tablespoons fresh lemon juice (about ½ a lemon)

2 teaspoons hot sauce

½ cup mayonnaise

½ cup cream cheese, at room temperature

8 ounces fresh lump crabmeat

½ teaspoon salt, plus more to your taste

½ cup panko

Preheat the oven to 375°F.

Combine the Cheddar, pimentos, Worcestershire, lemon juice, hot sauce, mayonnaise, cream cheese, crabmeat, and salt. Stir lightly until mixed sufficiently but not overstirred.

Spoon the mixture into an ovenproof serving dish (or two, depending on the size of the dish). Spread the panko evenly over the top. Bake for 20 minutes, until the crumbs are golden brown. If the crumbs aren't quite brown, turn the broiler on for the last minute or two. Cool for at least 10 minutes and then serve.

— HOW TO BRING IT —

You can prebake this and bring it to an event or bake it once you arrive. If you are prebaking and you want to serve it hot, bake it for 15 minutes and then an additional 5 minutes once you arrive. This recipe is fine served at room temperature but try not to serve straight from the refrigerator since the dip will have hardened.

Make sure to bring along something to dip with, such as bread or crackers on the side. You want something that is plain so that the flavors don't clash but sturdy enough to hold up (both physically and in terms of taste) to the weight of the dip. A sliced baguette or pita chips are two of my favorites.

Herbed Tzatziki

Tzatziki (pronounced tah-zee-key) is the best kind of make-ahead dish in that it gets better the longer it sits. Think of it as a cucumber and yogurt dip marinating in lemon, garlic, and herbs. This version has more herbs than you might see in other tzatziki recipes, but I think the herbs add a lot of freshness and flavor, making it more like a dip rather than just yogurt with some stuff thrown in. The other bonus to this dip is that it is quick to make and it can be served cold. It basically hits every prerequisite of a dish to bring along. If only everyone could learn to pronounce it properly, it would be perfect.

MAKES 3 CUPS (8 TO 10 SERVINGS)

1 large English cucumber

2 cups plain Greek yogurt

2 tablespoons chopped dill

2 tablespoons chopped parsley

2 tablespoons chopped mint

3 tablespoons fresh lemon juice

2 garlic cloves, minced finely or grated with a microplane

1 teaspoon salt

½ teaspoon freshly ground black pepper

Crusty bread or pita bread, toasted or warmed

Peel the cucumber, cut it in half lengthwise, and seed it, using a small spoon to scoop out the seeds from the center. Dice the cucumber into small ¼-inch pieces. Combine the cucumber, yogurt, herbs, lemon juice, garlic, salt, and pepper in a bowl and mix thoroughly, being careful not to crush the cucumbers. Serve cold with bread or pita on the side.

— HOW TO BRING IT —

This can be made up to 2 days ahead. If you like your tzatziki a little bit stronger, it actually benefits from sitting: the garlic and lemon become more pronounced. Just keep it in a sealed container in the refrigerator until you are ready to serve it; stir in any whey that collects on top.

— SUBSTITUTIONS —

This dish can be made with different fresh herbs if you have them on hand. You can also sprinkle smoked paprika on top when you serve it if you'd like a little more flavor and some color for the presentation. One thing not to substitute: make sure you really use Greek yogurt. Plain yogurt is a bit too loose.

Spicy Red Pepper Hummus

Hummus has become so embedded in our culinary consciousness that it is now considered a staple, and yet people rarely make it from scratch. It's not difficult to make, and homemade is so much more delicious than any prepared hummus. This version adds some spice to this otherwise creamy and savory dip that will make it feel like your own. You'll be surprised at how many people ask you for the recipe once you explain how easy it is to make at home.

**MAKES ABOUT 2 CUPS
(4 TO 6 SERVINGS)**

1 red bell pepper

1 (16-ounce) can chickpeas (also known as garbanzo beans)

Juice of 1 lemon

2 tablespoons tahini

3 garlic cloves, minced

1/2 teaspoon salt

1/4 teaspoon white pepper

1/2 teaspoon coriander

1/4 teaspoon cumin

1/4 teaspoon cayenne

2 tablespoons extra-virgin olive oil

If you have a gas stove, turn a stovetop burner on high heat or turn on the broiler. An outdoor grill also works well.

Use tongs to place the red pepper directly on or under the flame, and cook for 2 minutes on each side, approximately 8 minutes or until the pepper looks almost completely charred. Set aside to cool.

(recipe continues)

Drain the chickpeas but save ⅛ cup of the liquid from the can. Combine the chickpeas, lemon juice, tahini, garlic, salt, pepper, coriander, cumin, cayenne, and oil in a food processor or blender and blend until creamy and smooth. Make sure to take the time to scrape the inside of the canister a few times as you blend.

When the red pepper has cooled, scrape off the majority of the charred skin (as much as you can), core, seed, and dice the pepper, and fold into the hummus until smooth.

— HOW TO BRING IT —

This dip can be made up to a week ahead as long as it is stored in an airtight container in the refrigerator. Just give it a small stir before you put it out. I recommend serving it with pita bread or chips.

— SUBSTITUTIONS —

A lot of substitutes will work fine in this dish. Making the hummus base or the roasted red peppers from scratch is great, but you'll closely approximate the recipe if you buy either the hummus or roasted red pepper premade. The point here is to put a spin on your basic hummus with some texture and spice. Just blend the garlic, coriander, cumin, lemon, and red pepper into premade plain hummus, and you'll be all set.

Roasted red bell peppers are easily purchased: substitute 3/4 cup of drained, diced jarred peppers. You won't have quite the same texture but you will still get a lot of flavor.

If you can't find tahini you still could make this dish: while it adds a lot and I would encourage you to try and find it, in a pinch you can just add an extra tablespoon of olive oil. Just keep in mind that it won't come out quite the same. And if you don't want any spice, simply omit the cayenne.

The Best Artichoke Dip

I don't know how we got to a point where any dip including artichokes also had to include spinach. Why are we adding filler when what everyone wants is the artichokes? There's no filler here because every ingredient contributes for maximum flavor. You certainly could use fresh artichokes—and I would commend you if you did—but it's a lot of work for little reward. Just find the best plain packaged version you can. You can serve this at room temperature, but if possible try to serve warm.

MAKES 6 TO 8 SERVINGS

2 (14-ounce) cans or jars of artichoke hearts, drained, or 3 (9-ounce) packages of frozen artichoke hearts, thawed and drained

3/4 cup plus 2 tablespoons grated Parmesan cheese, divided

1/4 cup mayonnaise

1/4 cup sour cream

1/2 teaspoon ground black pepper

1/2 teaspoon salt

2 garlic cloves, diced

2 teaspoons hot sauce

2 teaspoons Worcestershire sauce

Juice of 1/2 a lemon

1 tablespoon parsley

Preheat the oven to 375°F.

Drain the artichokes and chop them into 1/4-inch pieces if necessary. Combine the artichokes with 3/4 cup Parmesan, mayonnaise, sour cream, pepper, salt, garlic, hot sauce, Worcestershire, and lemon juice. Transfer to a shallow 3-cup or 1-quart baking dish, smooth, and sprinkle the remaining 2 tablespoons of cheese on top.

Bake dip for 20 minutes. Remove from the oven and sprinkle the parsley on top. Serve warm with pita chips, or other chips strong enough to hold the dip.

NOTE: The total amount of artichoke hearts is flexible. Don't be afraid to add or subtract a few ounces to make things easy.

— HOW TO BRING IT —

You can assemble the artichoke dip a day ahead and bake just before serving. You might need to bake 5 to 10 minutes longer, depending on how cold it is. You can also fully assemble and bake the dip a day ahead. Just let it come to room temperature for 30 minutes before you reheat it for 5 to 10 minutes in an oven.

CHAPTER 3

Salads

Salads have to stand the literal test of time. Anything fussy will start to wilt before the crowd descends. The perfect portable salad should incorporate something hearty—a sturdy vegetable or beans or nuts—to ensure that it can hold its own alongside the main courses. Make sure that your ingredients are ultra fresh and of top quality. Without much cooking involved, each ingredient stands out more. This is especially true of a good olive oil or a ripe fruit or vegetable. Seasonality matters here.

Salads

———◆———

RECIPES

Tomato, Roasted Corn, and Feta Salad

This dish is so easy and flavorful it almost seems unfair. But there is one caveat: its simplicity can be its downfall. It's at its very best at the peak of summer with fresh corn and tomatoes: charring the corn makes it candy sweet. I started making this recipe during summer trips to my grandmother's house in New Hampshire, and I can assure you it didn't taste as good when I tried to make it in the dead of winter with hard out-of-season tomatoes. It is possible to make out of season—if you can find especially flavorful tomatoes.

MAKES 4 TO 6 SERVINGS

3 ears corn (about 2½ to 3 cups of kernels)

2 cups diced fresh tomatoes (about 2 pounds or 2 large tomatoes)

½ cup crumbled feta cheese

¼ cup diced basil

2 tablespoons fresh lemon juice (about ½ a lemon)

2 tablespoons extra-virgin olive oil

Dash of salt and freshly ground black pepper

If you have a gas stove, turn a stovetop burner to medium heat. Place the corn directly on top and turn approximately every minute until the corn is charred all the way around. If you do not have a gas stove, you can place the corn under the broiler in your oven, but be sure to turn every 10 to 20 seconds or so, to avoid overcooking it.

Allow the corn to fully cool and then cut the kernels from the cob. Combine the tomatoes, feta, basil, lemon juice, olive oil, salt, and pepper with the corn and serve.

— HOW TO BRING IT —

This can be made a day ahead but just make sure to toss it around again before serving. It holds up well as long as the tomatoes you use aren't too watery. Even if it gets a bit watery, there's an upside: you can dip crusty bread in the juices.

Three Bean Salad

This dish is the equivalent of a compulsion I have upon receiving a compliment on an article of my clothing: I just have to say that it was only twenty dollars, on sale, and I am so proud of how cheap it is. My husband finds this humiliating. It's the same concept here. People will devour this dish, exclaiming how delicious it is, and you won't be able to stop yourself from telling them how little work it was. You really should just smile and accept the compliments: there's something incredibly satisfying about a dish that sings without your even trying. I think the key is the raw garlic and rosemary—they give an unexpected kick to familiar flavors.

MAKES 6 SERVINGS

1 (15-ounce) can black beans (about 1½ cups), drained

1 (15-ounce) can cannellini beans (about 1½ cups), drained

1½ cups shelled edamame beans, cooked according to package instructions or unfrozen

½ cup diced shallots

¼ cup extra-virgin olive oil

1½ cups diced cucumbers

3 tablespoons fresh lemon juice

½ cup roughly chopped parsley

2 tablespoons finely chopped rosemary

2 garlic cloves, finely chopped or grated

1 teaspoon salt

Combine all ingredients in a bowl and toss well to coat. Serve.

— HOW TO BRING IT —

This dish can be made a day ahead and kept in the refrigerator. It can be served cold or at room temperature.

— SUBSTITUTIONS —

The varieties of beans here could be easily swapped: if you have fava beans, peas, even chickpeas, you could change them up. I like this particular combination but it's a forgiving dish that is great to do when you already have a few items on hand in your pantry. Just make sure not to swap the fresh herbs for dried ones: this dish uses plenty of canned ingredients and needs the pop of super fresh herbs.

Pear, Arugula, and Goat Cheese Salad

Sharp and sweet marry perfectly in this simple salad. The pear holds up against the arugula, and the goat cheese adds the balance that brings it all together. Topped with lemon zest, this is a lively offering for any outing.

MAKES 4 TO 6 SERVINGS

2 ripe pears, diced

4 cups arugula

3/4 cup crumbled goat cheese

1/2 cup sliced almonds

3 tablespoons extra-virgin olive oil

1 tablespoon balsamic vinegar

3 tablespoons fresh lemon juice

Dash of salt and freshly ground black pepper

1 tablespoon grated lemon zest

Toss the pears, arugula, goat cheese, and almonds together. Combine the olive oil, vinegar, lemon juice, salt, and pepper and slowly pour over the salad. Toss to combine, and finish by scattering the lemon zest on top.

— HOW TO BRING IT —

The lemon zest adds color and tang to the dish so try not to add it until right before you're going to serve the salad. If you're making this a full day ahead, keep the dressing separate from the salad and toss them together on arrival.

Shaved Carrots Salad

This salad is so different it will make you wonder why you don't make more salads without lettuce—because who needs it? This salad has texture and flavor galore, not to mention so many colors that it will be the centerpiece of any table and have everyone guessing until they bite into it. It's also one of the few cold-weather salads that evokes summertime sunshine.

MAKES 6 TO 8 SERVINGS

1 pound carrots

1 cup pomegranate seeds

Juice of 1 lemon

1 tablespoon extra-virgin olive oil

1 teaspoon sesame oil

1 teaspoon apple cider vinegar

1 cup chopped parsley

2 tablespoons sesame seeds

Dash of salt

Using a cheese slicer or a vegetable peeler, peel the carrots. Discard the first outer layer of every carrot but then make each thick peel into as long of a strand as you can. You won't be able to use the entirety of every carrot, but when you start to run out of room you can always flip the carrot over to the other side—just make sure to always discard that initial peel.

In a large salad bowl, combine the pomegranate seeds, lemon juice, olive oil, sesame oil, vinegar, parsley, sesame seeds, and salt with the carrots and toss until fully combined.

— SUBSTITUTIONS —

The length of the noodle-like peeled carrots here is up to you: long strands look beautiful but they are also slightly less easy to eat. If you are going to an event where there are plastic knives and no tables, you may want to chop the carrot strands a bit before serving. You can even use precut matchstick carrots in a pinch.

Buttermilk Broccoli Salad

This dish is sneakily classified as a salad only because it's served cold. Otherwise, it holds up nicely as a fully fledged vegetable side. It's hearty and flavorful, which makes it perfect for outdoor events or times when a dish might be sitting out a little longer. This is a very distant cousin of those mayonnaise-laden broccoli salads, but instead of weighing the vegetables down, the buttermilk adds a tang to the broccoli. It keeps the dish fresh and bright, which is key to any salad.

MAKES 4 SERVINGS

1 pound broccoli florets

8 ounces thick-cut bacon, cut into ½-inch cubes

1 garlic clove, finely minced

2 tablespoons extra-virgin olive oil

2 teaspoons apple cider vinegar

¼ cup finely chopped tarragon

¼ cup chopped parsley

½ cup buttermilk

½ cup slivered almonds

½ medium sweet onion (Vidalia preferred), cut into ¼-inch dice

⅓ cup crumbled blue cheese

Salt and freshly ground black pepper to taste

Make sure the broccoli florets are in roughly 1-inch pieces for cooking. Bring 1 to 2 inches of water to boil in a small pot with a steamer insert. If you do not have a steamer you can put a metal colander or strainer over boiling water and cover. It should work but might take a little longer. Steam the broccoli for approximately 4 minutes, or until the florets are cooked but still bright green and crisp. Drain and then plunge the florets into a bath of ice water. Drain again and set aside.

While the broccoli is cooking, sauté the bacon in a skillet on medium heat until cooked through, approximately 5 to 7 minutes, stirring frequently. In a large bowl, combine the garlic, olive oil, cider vinegar, tarragon, parsley, and buttermilk. Whisk until fully combined and then add the almonds, onion, and blue cheese along with the broccoli and bacon. Stir together until broccoli is fully coated. Add salt and pepper to taste.

— HOW TO BRING IT —

This salad does well either at room temperature or cold, so serve it as you prefer. The key here is to make sure your broccoli is cooked only to the point where it is crisp. If you overcook the broccoli, the whole dish starts to look and taste a bit sad, whereas it holds up beautifully with crisp bright green broccoli. The ice bath stops the cooking immediately; drain the broccoli right away and it will retain less water. If you want to make this a full day ahead, whisk the dressing together and store it separately from the broccoli salad, and toss them together the next day. Remove the salad from the fridge at least 10 minutes before serving, and stir it around to loosen it up a bit.

— SUBSTITUTIONS —

If you want to add an extra bit of flavor, you can toast the almonds before adding them. If you want to make this dish vegetarian, you can leave out the bacon.

Kale Salad with Carrot Ginger Dressing

Whenever I go to Japanese restaurants, I am often befuddled by the salads. They frequently pair an amazing carrot and ginger dressing with boring tasteless lettuce and a sad slice of cucumber. This dressing, an ingredient unto itself, deserves better. Here, it's paired with an equally delicious salad base. This salad will surprise and delight anyone sick of the same old lemon and olive oil dressings, and the vibrant colors are a bonus.

MAKES 6 SERVINGS

1 cup peeled and chopped carrots

1½ tablespoons chopped ginger

¼ cup minced shallots

1 tablespoon sherry vinegar

1 tablespoon soy sauce

3 tablespoons extra-virgin olive oil

¼ cup Parmesan cheese

5 cups roughly chopped kale
(lacinato preferred)

1 cup chopped pecans

1 cup diced apple

Dash of salt

Combine the carrots, ginger, shallots, vinegar, soy sauce, olive oil, and Parmesan cheese in a blender and blend until smooth. Toss the dressing with the kale, pecans, apple, and salt in a large bowl and serve.

— HOW TO BRING IT —

This salad holds up well for a day, but if you are keeping it in the fridge overnight, keep the dressing separate from the salad and mix when you're ready to eat.

Orange, Parsley, and Walnut Salad

Parsley is one of the most reliable additions to a dish, but what about making it take center stage? This salad can be the perfect light start to heavier dishes served in colder months, like shepherd's pie or baked chicken casserole, bringing a pop to winter meals. An ingredient as strong and sweet as an orange is a perfect companion for the parsley and the sharp crunch of endive.

MAKES 4 TO 6 SERVINGS

3 to 4 medium sized oranges (blood oranges or Cara cara, if in season)

2 cups chopped endive (preferably Belgian, about 2 endives)

1 cup chopped walnuts

2 cups chopped parsley

¼ cup extra-virgin olive oil

2 tablespoons sherry vinegar

Dash of salt

Peel and segment your oranges. If you want to go the extra mile, peel the oranges with a knife over the salad bowl to catch the juice. Remove all of the pith, and cut the fruit segments out between each membrane using the knife: this is called supreming, and it makes the salad look more polished. Set aside the membranes of the oranges for the dressing: they still have plenty of juice.

Toss the oranges with the endive, walnuts, and parsley. In a smaller bowl combine the olive oil and sherry vinegar. Squeeze out any excess liquid from the orange membranes and then whisk the dressing together. Toss the salad with the dressing, add a dash of salt, and serve.

— SUBSTITUTIONS —

Blood and Cara cara oranges are usually only available in winter, so feel free to change the variety if you find they aren't available. Make sure to check the quality of the oranges you are purchasing though: mealy, off-season citrus will make the entire dish lose its character. You want fragrant oranges that aren't too firm. You can also substitute other lettuces for endive, but choose a sharper variety (like arugula or radicchio) to keep the contrast with the sweetness of the orange. Lastly, if you can't find sherry vinegar, you can use red wine vinegar instead.

Potato Salad with Soy Vinaigrette

I know what you're thinking: Why is potato salad even in the salad section? But that's where you've been going wrong about potato salad all these years. This is not your grandmother's heavy mayo-laden potato salad (no offense to your grandmother). More than just a plate filler, this lighter version feels bright and flavorful and—dare I say?—fun.

MAKES 4 TO 6 SERVINGS

1½ pounds small red potatoes or a mix of tricolored potatoes (about 15 to 20 potatoes)

2 tablespoons soy sauce

2 tablespoons fresh lemon juice (about ½ a lemon)

2 tablespoons mayonnaise

1 tablespoon chopped tarragon

1 red bell pepper, diced

¼ cup diced red onion

¼ cup diced scallions (about 3 scallions)

1 cup chopped tomato

Dash of salt

Add the potatoes to a pot of water and bring to a boil. Cook for 8 to 15 minutes, depending on the size of your potatoes, until they are softened but still with a bit of bite. Strain and run cold water over them to cool.

Once they are cool, cut them into 1-inch pieces. Combine the soy sauce, lemon juice, mayonnaise, and tarragon. Add the potatoes to the pepper, onion, scallions, tomato, and salt and combine with the dressing.

Tomato Orzo Salad

When pasta is included in a salad, it often supersedes the vegetable part of the equation. But really, it should complement the dish: you want greens and other ingredients to round out the pasta, offering texture, flavor, and lightness. This salad has all of those components, with a surprise ingredient. That small versatile pasta, orzo, with feta and spinach is a classic combination, but the addition of fresh tomatoes and tomato paste takes it to a different level. The depth of tomato flavor combined with the freshness of the tomatoes makes it a perfect salad for any season.

MAKES 6 TO 8 SERVINGS

8 ounces (1 cup) orzo pasta

1 tablespoon tomato paste

2 cups chopped baby spinach

1 cup crumbled feta cheese

2 cups halved cherry tomatoes

1/2 cup chopped basil leaves

1/4 cup chopped scallions

1 1/2 cups chopped cucumber (about 1 medium cucumber)

2 tablespoons balsamic vinegar

2 tablespoons extra-virgin olive oil

Dash of salt

Bring a salted pot of water to a boil. Add the orzo and cook 8 to 10 minutes, or until al dente (it should still have a bit of bite). Drain and rinse with cold water.

In a bowl combine the orzo with the tomato paste until fully coated: make sure it is completely cool. Add the spinach, feta, tomatoes, basil, scallions, cucumber, vinegar, olive oil, and salt, and carefully stir together until it is evenly combined.

— HOW TO BRING IT —

This salad is fine cold or at room temperature. You can store it for up to 2 days covered in the fridge; just be sure to give it a stir before serving. If your tomatoes are on the watery side, you may not want to store it for more than a day.

Snap Pea Salad with Parmesan and Bacon

Nothing makes a salad quite as universally beloved as the addition of bacon. Add in a bit of cheese, and you'd be forgiven for wondering how this still counts as a salad. But the crispness of the snap peas stands out among these strong ingredients. Hearty snap peas are a good replacement for lettuce or other greens because they don't wilt. This dish makes for an unctuous option when you want to add just a bit of meat to the proceedings.

MAKES 6 SERVINGS

4 ounces bacon

5 cups snap peas (about 1¼ pounds)

½ cup grated Parmesan cheese

Juice of 1 lemon

¼ cup extra-virgin olive oil

Dash of salt and freshly ground black pepper

Bring a pot of salted water to a boil and place a skillet over medium-high heat. Add the bacon to the skillet, stirring occasionally until cooked, about 7 to 10 minutes (whether you want the bacon crispy or not is your choice, so just watch the timing).

While the bacon is cooking, add ice and water into a bowl large enough to hold all the snap peas. Trim the snap peas and add them to the boiling water for 1 minute. Immediately drain the snap peas and put them in the bowl of ice water. After another minute drain and set the snap peas aside to dry.

When the bacon is done cooking remove from the skillet onto paper towels to cool. Once the bacon is cool, chop into small pieces, approximately ¼ inch. Toss the bacon with the snap peas, Parmesan cheese, lemon juice, olive oil, salt, and pepper. Toss together to combine.

Plum and Cucumber Salad

Sometimes the best combinations are the most surprising. Plums may not be your first thought for combining with lime and chili flakes, but it's one you won't soon forget. It's an unusual way to enjoy the all-too-brief plum season at the height of summer. And as a bonus, this salad only takes 10 minutes to make.

MAKES 8 TO 10 SERVINGS

4 to 5 large ripe plums, diced (about 4 cups)

2 large English cucumbers, sliced into ¼-inch disks (about 4 cups)

3 tablespoons fresh lime juice (about 2 to 3 limes)

¼ cup extra-virgin olive oil

½ cup finely chopped cilantro

½ tablespoon dried chili flakes

Dash of salt

Combine all ingredients and serve.

NOTE: This dish is spicy. If you'd like it to be less so, you can easily cut the amount of chili flakes in half. Remember, you can't take spicy out, so it may be wise to start with half the amount and gradually add more. The spice and salt ratio is also important: make sure to add a bit more salt as needed depending on how much spice you are using.

— SUBSTITUTIONS —

This dish is also great with peaches. Just substitute the same number of peaches for plums.

Herb Salad

When did herbs get relegated to the assisting role? Why don't we ever let them shine in all their glory? This simple salad packed with zing brings herbs into the limelight and is the perfect vehicle if you happen to have a crisper drawer of herbs begging to be used up. It's a wonderful light accompaniment for any rich meal, in any season.

MAKES 6 SERVINGS

1 cup basil

1 cup parsley

1 cup chives

1 cup tarragon

1 cup mint

3 cups arugula

Juice of 1 lemon

1 teaspoon whole grain mustard

¼ cup extra-virgin olive oil

Dash of salt

Roughly chop the herbs and combine them in a bowl. In a separate bowl, whisk together the lemon juice, mustard, olive oil, and salt. Add the dressing to the herbs to taste: start with half of the dressing, adding more as needed.

— HOW TO BRING IT —

This salad can be chopped and combined a day ahead but store the dressing and salad separately if you're holding this for more than a few hours.

— SUBSTITUTIONS —

If you can't find one or two of the herbs you can always substitute with others: just keep the ratios the same. You can also add in additional herbs. But be mindful of the strength of any herb and whether it'll change the overall tenor of the dish and introduce it gradually. Remember, you can always add more but you can't take out.

Brussels Sprouts Salad

Brussels sprouts have somehow become fashionable only when served as a roasted side dish. But the formerly controversial vegetable has more to offer than just one simple preparation. This salad takes the benefits of roasting but lightens it up for a cold salad. Although kiwi might seem like a surprising addition, the pop of the fruit adds an extra dimension that pulls the Brussels sprouts into lighter territory. It might be a few extra steps more than your typical salad, but the result is worth it.

MAKES 6 TO 8 SERVINGS

6 cups Brussels sprouts (about 2 pounds)

4 tablespoons extra-virgin olive oil

Dash of salt

2 tablespoons Dijon mustard

Juice of 1 lemon

½ cup pine nuts

1 cup diced apples

½ cup diced kiwi

Preheat the oven to 400°F.

Trim and halve the Brussels sprouts. Line a sheet pan with aluminum foil and spread the Brussels sprouts out on the tray. Sprinkle with half the olive oil and the dash of salt, and roast in the oven for 12 to 15 minutes. Turn on the oven's broiler and place the Brussels sprouts on a rack close to the flame. Cook for an additional 2 to 4 minutes until the Brussels sprouts start to brown.

Remove from the oven and let cool. Once the sprouts are cooled, chop them finely until they resemble salad leaves rather than a whole vegetable. In a bowl, combine the remaining olive oil, mustard, and lemon juice. Whisk to combine. Add the dressing to the Brussels sprouts along with the nuts, apples, and kiwi. Stir to combine.

— HOW TO BRING IT —

This salad is a bit susceptible to wilting since the Brussels sprouts are already cooked with olive oil, but since they are so hearty, usually just a quick toss will bring them back to life. Don't store the salad and dressing separately because the lemon juice will stop the apples from oxidizing and turning brown. So just be mindful of time with this one: it *will* hold for two days, but one is better.

Frisée with Eggs and Bacon

When I was in college, I was a waitress at a restaurant that had a version of this salad. All the regulars ordered it, and for the life of me I could not understand why. After all, who wants to eat a salad that barely has anything in it? But then one day I tried it and realized that its simplicity was its strength. There was something about the way the egg yolk clung to the frisée leaves that made it all come together. Ever since, I've been making this version for myself. I've made a few changes, as I've brought it to parties and dinners over the years: the poached egg goes in the dressing and then we add soft-boiled eggs to the salad itself. Frisée is extra sturdy and retains its crunch until the salad bowl is empty. And the raw garlic and shallots make it so flavorful that you'll have guests wondering why they keep going back for seconds and thirds of a seemingly basic salad.

MAKES 4 TO 6 SERVINGS

4 large eggs, still cold from the fridge

1 teaspoon white vinegar

4 ounces bacon, cut into ¼-inch cubes

2 tablespoons sherry vinegar

2 garlic cloves, grated or finely minced

2 tablespoons finely chopped shallots (about 1 large shallot)

3 tablespoons extra-virgin olive oil

4 cups frisée

Dash of salt

Bring a small pot of water to a roiling simmer on medium high: make sure not to let it boil (this is the secret to perfect poached eggs and it has never failed me). Crack one of the eggs into a cup or ramekin so no eggshells get in the pot. Add the vinegar to the pot of water and tip in the egg. Let it cook for 3 minutes undisturbed. Remove the egg with a slotted spoon and set aside to cool.

Bring a pot of water to a boil (feel free to use the poaching water), and place a sauté pan on medium-high heat. Add the bacon to the sauté pan. Cook the bacon for 5 minutes, or until it is cooked to your desired doneness (chewy or crisp, however you like it), then set it on a paper towel.

(recipe continues)

While the bacon is cooking, add the remaining eggs to the pot of boiling water and set a timer for exactly 6 minutes: this will yield yolks that are just firm but also slightly soft and a bit runny in the centers. When the eggs are finished, remove with a slotted spoon and run under cold water for 30 seconds (or you can place them in an ice water bath if you prefer).

To make the dressing, combine the poached egg with the sherry vinegar, garlic, shallots, and olive oil. Make sure to use a fork to break up the poached egg and combine fully with the rest of the ingredients.

Peel the soft-boiled eggs and cut them into quarters. Combine three-quarters of the dressing with the frisée. Add the bacon and eggs on top, and pour the remaining dressing on, along with the dash of salt.

— HOW TO BRING IT —

This salad can be made up to a day ahead but store the dressing separately and combine only before serving, to keep the frisée leaves from wilting. It's preferable to serve this salad at room temperature, but it won't do much harm to serve it straight out of the fridge.

Peach and Prosciutto Salad

I ordered a peach and prosciutto salad on a trip to Lake Como in Italy, and to my delight it was not merely a few pieces of peaches and prosciutto thrown on top of a pile of lettuce. On the contrary, lettuce was barely involved: just the juicy peaches and the perfect prosciutto wrapped together. My brother tried to argue with me that the dish was not really a salad. But I loved it because it inverted the usual salad experience by emphasizing the most delicious ingredients. This re-creation of that salad is done in that same spirit. Why not bring the ingredients people want most to the center of the dish?

MAKES 6 TO 8 SERVINGS

4 ripe peaches

8 slices good-quality prosciutto

1½ tablespoons balsamic vinegar

1½ tablespoons extra-virgin olive oil

¼ cup chopped basil leaves

Salt and freshly ground black pepper to taste

Cut the peaches in half and take out the pits. Chop into ½-inch pieces. Cut the prosciutto into small pieces as well. Combine in a bowl with the vinegar, olive oil, basil, salt, and pepper.

Cauliflower Salad with Lime and Turmeric

Sometimes an occasion calls for brightness. This salad embodies that while also being hearty enough to feel like a substantial addition to the meal. Turmeric has been lauded for its supposed health properties, but I love it for its subtle, lovely bitterness. It brings balance to the lime and adds a beautiful color. This simple salad will stand out both visually and in flavor.

MAKES 4 SERVINGS

1 large head cauliflower (about 2 pounds)

1 tablespoon extra-virgin olive oil

Dash of salt

1/2 teaspoon turmeric

3 cups arugula

1/4 cup fresh lime juice (about 2 limes)

1 cup pepitas or sunflower seeds

Preheat the oven to 450°F.

Chop the cauliflower into small florets and place them on a sheet pan. Drizzle the olive oil on the cauliflower and add a dash of salt. Roast in the oven for 20 to 25 minutes, turning once or twice, until the cauliflower is golden brown.

Remove from the oven and set aside to cool. Once the cauliflower is cool, chop it into smaller bite-size pieces and toss in a bowl with the turmeric, and then add the arugula, lime juice, and seeds and toss.

— HOW TO BRING IT —

This salad can be made ahead, but store the arugula separately—it wilts quickly if dressed too early. You can toss all the other ingredients with the dressing together at least a day ahead if needed, but save the arugula until the last minute before serving.

CHAPTER 4
Casseroles,

Pasta, and Tarts

Casseroles and tarts are the essence of a shared meal. These satisfying dishes pack flavor into a single pan. They transport easily and often don't need to be reheated on arrival. The key to a great casserole or tart is to pick ingredients that won't get soggy or stale if they have to sit out a bit. Temperature is also important. If you're serving a dish cold, then great: cook it fully, refrigerate, transport, and you're set. But if you are reheating, it's better to initially undercook the dish, and then finish browning or crisping it when you reheat. Even the best casserole can go sideways if it's been heated too long.

Casseroles, Pasta, and Tarts

—•—

RECIPES

Pistachio and Anchovy Pasta

Sometimes the best meals happen when you least expect it. My husband and I spent a few weeks in Italy one summer, with almost every day packed with reservations for meals. But our favorite dish came when we stopped in the town of Siena for a break during a drive through the countryside. Ready to eat, we sat down at the first restaurant that had outdoor seating and accepted that it was going to be a simple, quick meal. How wrong we were. We ordered a pasta that combined anchovies with pistachios, and suddenly our world opened to a whole new flavor. When I came home, it was the first recipe I tried to muster up in my American kitchen. It's a surprising flavor that will stick with you long after you've put your fork down.

MAKES 4 TO 6 SERVINGS

8 ounces orecchiette or other small pasta

1 cup unsalted shelled pistachios

4 tablespoons extra-virgin olive oil

1 (2-ounce) jar or tin of anchovies

1 teaspoon crushed red pepper flakes

½ cup freshly grated Parmesan cheese

½ cup coarsely chopped flat-leaf parsley

Salt to taste

Bring a pot of salted water to a boil. Add the pasta and cook for 8 minutes or until the pasta is cooked but still a bit al dente.

While the pasta is cooking, combine the pistachios, olive oil, and anchovies in a blender until almost smooth but with still just a little bit of texture. Combine the blended mixture with the red pepper flakes, Parmesan cheese, and parsley in a large serving bowl, stirring to make a sauce.

Drain the pasta and immediately combine with the sauce. Add salt to taste.

— HOW TO BRING IT —

This dish can be served immediately or it can be gently reheated in an oven. Try not to add too much heat too fast or the cheese will lose its texture and the pasta could overcook. It also does fine at room temperature if needed.

Baked Chicken and Pasta Casserole

Certain ingredients are basic for a reason. Chicken and pasta will please even the pickiest of eaters, but just because we are combining two dependable favorites doesn't mean this recipe is boring. On the contrary it will be the comfort food that draws everyone in for seconds. The key to any baked pasta dish is to not to overcook the main ingredients: any baked pasta should be slightly underdone before you assemble the casserole. Baking brings everything together. This isn't a recipe to be served at room temperature so plan to reheat just before serving.

MAKES 4 TO 6 SERVINGS

2 cups penne

1 tablespoon extra-virgin olive oil

3 garlic cloves, minced

1 diced medium white onion

12 to 16 ounces chicken breast, diced (about 2 cups)

2 (14-ounce) cans diced tomatoes (about 3½ cups)

¼ cup ricotta cheese

1 cup Parmesan cheese

2 cups spinach

1 large egg, beaten

4 tablespoons chopped fresh basil

2 tablespoons fresh thyme

2 teaspoons salt

Preheat the oven to 500°F.

Bring a salted pot of water to boil and drop your penne in to cook for 5 minutes. Strain and set aside: the pasta should be only partially cooked and still extremely al dente.

Heat olive oil in a saucepan on medium-high heat. Add the garlic and onion and cook for 5 minutes, stirring a few times. Add the chicken breast and cook an additional 5 minutes: your goal is to only cook the chicken halfway.

Combine the tomatoes, ricotta, Parmesan, spinach, egg, basil, thyme, and salt in a bowl and stir carefully. Add the pasta, garlic, onions, and chicken, gently combine, and then pour into a baking dish. Bake for 10 minutes and serve.

— HOW TO BRING IT —

The biggest tip here is to not overcook. You can make this in advance up to the stage where it is ready to be baked. Let it cool down completely, cover it, and put it in the fridge for up to 24 hours. If you are cooking straight from the fridge, you may want to add a few minutes to the cooking time.

If you are traveling with this dish, do some planning. Ask the host whether you can use the oven at 500°F. If they are cooking other things, you might only have access to 350°F or 400°F. Bake for 20 minutes at a lower temperature, or until the dish is bubbling around the sides. You may not have the same browning on top, but the flavors will be similar.

The Quickest, Most Flavorful Bolognese

There's nothing home cooks love more than telling you all about how many hours they labored over a sauce. It's like a badge of honor: the longer it took, the better it obviously must be. But these labors of love can often feel like a punishment. Surely there has to be a better way. I find there are ways to create flavor without the extensive cooking times. My secret ingredients are anchovies and soy sauce: they add that oomph that would otherwise require browning or hours of cooking. Don't be scared of anchovies: their flavor melts into the sauce and you won't even realize they are there. If you are cooking for someone who doesn't like them, you can easily get away without mentioning your secret ingredient—your guest (or family member) will never know.

MAKES 4 TO 6 SERVINGS

2 tablespoons unsalted butter

1 medium white onion, chopped

4 garlic cloves, minced

2 pounds ground beef

8 anchovies

2 tablespoons tomato paste

2 tablespoons soy sauce

1 (28-ounce) can chopped tomatoes

2 tablespoons dried basil

Dash of salt

1 pound thick, short pasta, like a rigatoni or farfalle

Melt the butter in a pot on medium-high heat. Add the onions and garlic and cook for 5 minutes, or until the onions start to look translucent.

Add the beef and cook an additional 5 to 7 minutes, or until it starts to brown. Try not to stir too much once it gets going to ensure that the beef browns, but do break it up into small pieces at the beginning of the cooking process (you don't want chunks).

While the beef is cooking, mash the anchovies either with an immersion blender or in a bowl using a fork: you want to break it up as much as possible. Add the anchovies, tomato paste, soy sauce, tomatoes, basil, and salt to the beef and onions, and bring to a simmer. Cook 10 minutes more, stirring occasionally. Taste and adjust seasonings as necessary. If you used a particularly fatty beef, feel free to drain off some of the fat if it starts to collect.

While the sauce is cooking, bring a large pot of salted water to a boil. Add the pasta and cook according to the package instructions (usually 6 to 10 minutes). When it is done to your liking, drain. Add the pasta to the sauce and serve.

NOTE: Don't store the cooked pasta separately from the sauce. Keep it all together: it's easier, and it tastes better.

— HOW TO BRING IT —

You want to serve this hot. If you make it ahead of time, let it cool to room temperature and then refrigerate. When you are ready to serve, you can reheat in the oven at 350°F or on the stovetop for 10 to 15 minutes. Stir as you go. You can add a bit more tomato paste and a *touch* of water to reconstitute it.

Hash Brown Casserole

Hash browns are the perfect diner food that you never make at home. Although you can make them at home, they generally need to be served immediately for that crisp out-of-the-pan taste. This dish, however, manages to convey that comforting hash brown flavor but has enough substance to hold up over time. Though neither healthy nor aesthetically pleasing, this casserole is a surefire crowd pleaser. Nothing is quite as comforting as the simplicity of potatoes and Cheddar cheese.

MAKES 8 SERVINGS

6 large russet potatoes

1 cup chicken stock

12 ounces Cheddar cheese, grated
(about 1½ cups)

½ cup sour cream

1 diced yellow onion

2 eggs

2 poblano chiles, diced with seeds and stem
removed

2 teaspoons salt, plus more as needed

½ teaspoon freshly ground black pepper

¼ cup thinly sliced spring onions

Preheat the oven to 350°F.

Peel the potatoes and then shred them on a box grater using the largest holes. Wrap the potatoes in paper towels (or cheesecloth) and squeeze out as much moisture as possible. You can also let the potatoes sit before you squeeze them as some of the liquid will start to leach out. Place the potatoes on a micro-waveable plate and cook in the microwave on the highest setting for 1 minute and 30 seconds. Rest them on paper towels to cool and soak up the last of the moisture.

Set aside approximately 1 of the 6 grated potatoes (about 1 cup). Combine the stock, cheese, sour cream, yellow onion, eggs, poblano chiles, salt, pepper, and spring onions with the remaining potatoes in a bowl and pour into a 13 x 9-inch (or similar) glass baking dish. Sprinkle the reserved grated potato on top and then season with additional salt and pepper.

Cover with foil and bake for 30 minutes. Remove the foil and cook for an additional 10 minutes. Turn the broiler on high and cook for an additional 2 to 3 minutes until the top is brown and crispy. Sprinkle the spring onions on top and serve.

— HOW TO BRING IT —

This dish is better hot than not, although it does just fine as long as it stays a bit warm. If you will be traveling with it, skip the broiler step and do that on arrival: just be sure you take it out of the fridge with enough time for it to come to room temperature before you put it under the broiler. It will hold for a day in the fridge, saving the broiler step until right before serving: the crispy potatoes on top really bring this dish together so don't skip it.

— SUBSTITUTIONS —

This is a dish where meat is easily added if you would like it: cooked bacon or crumbled sausage obviously marry well with hash browns and both hold up over time. Similarly, if you want to go completely vegetarian, you could replace the chicken stock with vegetable stock.

Red Wine Pasta

Pasta often relies on other ingredients to add color. In this dish, however, the pasta is the star. I once encountered a version of this recipe in a restaurant and thought that color had been added to the pasta dough itself. But you can make this magical burgundy pasta with whatever dried pasta is in your pantry. Spaghetti is used in this recipe, but almost any pasta size or shape will do: the concept remains the same. The wine adds an earthy fruit flavor to the dish, and the simple addition of pine nuts, feta, and parsley brings another dimension.

MAKES 6 TO 8 SERVINGS

4 tablespoons unsalted butter, divided

3 garlic cloves, diced

1 (750 ml) bottle light red wine, such as Beaujolais

1 pound spaghetti or other pasta

1 cup pine nuts

1½ cups crumbled feta cheese

Juice of ½ a lemon

1 cup fresh chopped basil

Salt to taste

Find a pan wide enough to hold the uncooked spaghetti. Melt 2 tablespoons of the butter in the pan on medium-high heat and add the garlic. Cook for 3 to 4 minutes until the garlic just starts to brown.

Add the red wine and 1 cup of water, and bring to a boil. Add the spaghetti and reduce heat to a rapid simmer. Cook the pasta until the wine has been absorbed, approximately 8 to 10 minutes (or according to your particular pasta's instructions), stirring occasionally.

Depending on the pasta you are using, you may need to add up to 2 more cups of water as you cook. If the pasta has absorbed the liquid but still isn't quite done to your liking: add another half a cup at a time until it is done.

Add the remaining 2 tablespoons of the butter in the last minute or two before the pasta is done. Remove from the heat and toss with the pine nuts, feta cheese, lemon, and basil. Add salt to taste.

— HOW TO BRING IT —

The way you handle this recipe depends on whether you want to serve it hot or cold. If you are serving it cold, you can just refrigerate it after cooking and serve it as is up to 2 days later. If you are serving it hot, save the feta, lemon juice, and basil for whenever you are serving it. Cook the pasta fully and store separately; keep the pine nuts, feta, and parsley in another container. To reheat, place the cooked pasta in a skillet with a tablespoon of butter and bring back up to temperature, and then mix in the remaining ingredients.

Pesto Vinaigrette Pasta

I had a friend who loved pesto and ate it constantly, but she always bought a jar instead of making it. When I asked her why, she said, "Pine nuts are too expensive." It's true that pine nuts can be very expensive, but the good news is that you can substitute other nuts. Here I use almonds, and to loosen up the pesto and provide a tangy flavor, I turned it into a vinaigrette with additional lemon and a little mustard. It takes only a few more seconds than opening a jar.

MAKES 4 SERVINGS

1 cup basil

Juice of 1 lemon

3 garlic cloves

½ cup extra-virgin olive oil

2 teaspoons Dijon mustard

¼ cup Parmesan cheese

¼ cup almonds

Salt and freshly ground black pepper to taste

1 pound rigatoni or another thick pasta

Put the basil, lemon juice, garlic, oil, mustard, Parmesan, almonds, and salt and pepper to taste in a blender, and blend until smooth.

Bring a pot of salted water to a boil. Add the pasta and cook according to the package instructions (about 8 to 10 minutes or until al dente). Drain the pasta and combine with the sauce.

— HOW TO BRING IT —

This dish works well hot or cold and can be stored for up to 2 days in the refrigerator. If you are reheating, undercook it just a touch and reheat in the oven or on the stovetop. You can add a touch more water to help it reconstitute, but try not to cook it too long. If you are making the dish just before serving, don't undercook the pasta; just make sure you are using a hearty enough pasta so it doesn't "wilt" while you're transporting it.

— SUBSTITUTIONS —

If you have someone with a nut issue, this sauce works fine without the almonds. It will lose a bit of texture and flavor, but it's an easy change. This pesto can also be used as a topping on meats, sandwiches, or crackers.

Portobello Mushroom and Herb Casserole

This is one of those kitchen-sink dishes where you basically just throw a bunch of ingredients together and somehow it makes something beautiful. It's a hearty vegetarian main course option that will also be rich enough to please even the meat eaters. Between the smokiness of the paprika, the umami in the soy, and the acidity in the lemon, you have the perfect combination.

MAKES 6 TO 8 SERVINGS.

1 large white onion, diced

3 shallots, finely chopped

3 large garlic cloves, diced

1 tablespoon extra-virgin olive oil

1 (14-ounce) can cannellini beans, drained of their liquid

4 cups chopped portobello mushrooms (about 4 mushroom caps)

1/3 cup chopped walnuts

1/3 cup chopped parsley

2 tablespoons chopped sage

1 tablespoon chopped fresh oregano

1/2 teaspoon smoked paprika

1 tablespoon soy sauce

Juice of 1 lemon

1 1/2 cups goat cheese

1 teaspoon salt

Preheat the oven to 350°F.

Place a skillet on medium-high heat. Add the onion, shallots, garlic, and oil, and cook for 5 to 7 minutes until the onions are translucent. Scrape the onion mixture into a bowl and add the beans, mushrooms, walnuts, parsley, sage, oregano, paprika, soy sauce, lemon juice, goat cheese, and salt. Stir to combine.

Transfer the mixture to a baking dish and place in the oven for 20 minutes, stirring halfway through to help the beans soak up some of the liquid. Serve warm.

— HOW TO BRING IT —

This dish can be stored for up to 2 days. Be sure to stir it around a bit before reheating. Some of the juices and moisture may have come out of the mushrooms, but once it is all warmed back up, it will be fine. Place in a 350°F oven for 5 to 10 minutes (depending on how cold the dish is) and serve warm.

Baked Eggplant Towers

I've always loved a dramatic presentation, and this one certainly does the job. These beautiful little stacks are like a single serving of healthy eggplant Parmesan. The trick here is in pan-searing the eggplant slices, instead of baking or frying them and having them go a bit mushy. This technique brings them to the edge of crispy. It's a main course for a vegetarian or a perfectly portioned side dish for anyone else.

MAKES 4 TO 6 SERVINGS

2 large eggplants, or 4 small ones

3 large tomatoes, or 6 small ones

2 cups crumbled feta cheese

1 cup chopped basil

Dash of salt

Dash of extra-virgin olive oil and balsamic vinegar (optional)

Preheat the oven to 450°F.

Cut the eggplant into ½- to 1-inch-thick round slices, depending on your preference. Place a large nonstick pan on medium-high heat (if you don't have a nonstick pan, you can lightly spray any skillet with nonstick spray, but just keep it very light so as not to add moisture to the eggplant). Once it has heated up, place the eggplant rounds on the pan and cook in batches for 4 minutes on each side; they should brown substantially.

When each batch is complete, sprinkle salt on the face-up side of the eggplant and cool on a baking rack above a sheet pan.

While the eggplant is cooking, cut the tomatoes into ½-inch-thick slices. When the eggplant is cool, arrange the first layers of the eggplant on a sheet pan lined with aluminum foil. Stack a layer of tomato slices on top of the eggplant rounds, then sprinkle on some feta, basil, and salt. Add an eggplant slice on top of that and repeat with the tomato, feta, basil, and salt. Add a final layer of eggplant on top to finish the stack.

Place in the oven for 10 minutes or until the cheese begins to melt. Remove from the oven and cool. You can drizzle the stacks with a bit of olive oil and balsamic vinegar if desired.

— HOW TO BRING IT —

This dish can be served hot or at room temperature. You can refrigerate before serving as long as the eggplants are covered tightly and then placed in an oven just before serving, but keep in mind that eggplants coming straight from a fridge might need to cook a bit longer. If you are traveling far and are nervous about them toppling over en route, you can always keep the parts separate and arrange them on-site before sticking them in the oven. In either scenario, you should only do the olive oil and balsamic drizzle right before serving.

— SUBSTITUTIONS —

Don't be afraid to use the grill here if you have one: you can grill the eggplant, but just watch them carefully so that they don't burn.

Grits Casserole

I grew up in Charleston, South Carolina, so grits are a way of life for me. A lot of people who didn't grow up with grits think they are a niche starch, but they are actually as versatile and comforting as rice or pasta and quite easy to make. Give grits a chance, and you won't regret it. This casserole gives grits a bit of staying power and makes it easier to serve them. My secret weapon is bacon grease: it adds an unctuous, smoky flavor to the dish that tips it over the edge. This flavorful dish may convert you into thinking of grits as a practical, everyday starch.

MAKES 6 TO 8 SERVINGS

2 cups whole milk

½ cup salted butter, cut into 1-inch pieces, divided

2 cups stone-ground grits

4 ounces thick-cut bacon, cut into ½-inch pieces

1 teaspoon salt

8 ounces sharp Cheddar cheese, grated, divided (about 2 cups)

3 large eggs, beaten

Preheat the oven to 350°F.

Bring 5 cups water and the milk to a boil with half of the butter in a heavy pot on medium-high heat. Add the grits and stir continuously until the mixture returns to a boil. Reduce the heat, cover, and stir frequently for 10 to 15 minutes until the grits have thickened but are still a bit al dente to taste (your brand of grits really could make a difference here so always keep tasting as you cook in case it cooks more quickly).

While the grits are cooking, cook the bacon in a skillet on medium-high heat for 4 to 7 minutes until cooked through but not yet crispy. Set aside.

When the grits are done, remove the pot from the heat, add the remaining butter, salt, and 1½ cups of the cheese to the mixture until incorporated. Add the bacon, all the bacon grease from the pan, and the eggs, and stir quickly and vigorously so the eggs don't cook before being incorporated.

Pour the mixture into a 13 x 9 or 8-inch baking dish, and sprinkle the remaining cheese over the top. Bake in the oven for 45 minutes to 1 hour or until the top is golden.

— HOW TO BRING IT —

This dish can be made a day ahead and refrigerated. You could cook it for a bit less time (30 to 45 minutes) and then reheat in an oven at the same temperature for 15 to 20 minutes.

— SUBSTITUTION —

You can also easily make this into a vegetarian dish by eliminating the bacon and bacon grease. I think bacon adds a special quality to the dish, but you wouldn't ruin everything by taking it out.

Spicy Brussels Sprouts Tart

Brussels sprouts have an undeserved bad rap. People often don't appreciate how they can pull a dish together by giving it some weight and texture. I would know since they are my mother's favorite food, and I've been coming up with ways to make them more interesting ever since I was a child. This tart relies on the hearty nature of Brussels sprouts, but it also aims to convert skeptics: the addition of bacon, cheese, and a bit of spice helps the cause.

MAKES 6 SERVINGS

1 pie crust (store bought or on page 119)

1 large yellow onion, diced

4 ounces thick-cut bacon, cut into ½-inch cubes

3 garlic cloves, finely diced

2 cups grated Brussels sprouts

1 tablespoon balsamic vinegar

½ teaspoon red pepper flakes

½ cup ricotta

½ cup freshly grated Parmesan cheese

2 eggs, beaten

1 teaspoon salt

Preheat the oven to 400°F.

Place the pie crust in a pie pan and crimp the edges. Bake for 5 to 7 minutes, until it has started to harden and brown lightly. Remove it from the oven and cool.

Meanwhile, place a nonstick pan on medium-high heat. Add the onion, bacon, and garlic cloves to the pan and sauté for 5 minutes until the bacon is almost completely cooked through and the onions have started to brown (try not to stir too much). Remove the pan from the heat and allow it to cool a bit (if your particular brand of bacon has a ton of fat you can drain some of the fat from the pan if you prefer).

Combine the cooked ingredients with all the remaining ingredients and pour them into the pie shell. Bake for 25 to 30 minutes until the center of the tart has set and the top has started to brown a bit. Cool at least 10 minutes before serving.

— HOW TO BRING IT —

This dish is easy to make ahead just as long as you keep the timing in mind. It's better when hot so undercook it a bit if you are making it ahead and then put it back in the oven for 10 to 15 minutes (depending on how cold it was when you put it in) to make sure it comes back up to temperature.

— SUBSTITUTIONS —

This recipe is called spicy for a reason. It won't be overwhelming but it definitely has a kick. If you are concerned about the spice, feel free to reduce the red pepper flakes by half or even eliminate them.

Shepherd's Pie

I went to college in Scotland and I was introduced to shepherd's pie by my roommate's mother, who would make it every time I came back from a visit to the US. It was my little reminder that I had journeyed back, and it always felt like the most comforting food possible. Unlike the more familiar pot pie, shepherd's pie has mashed potatoes on top, giving it a fluffy texture without the potential pitfalls of a fussy pastry crust. Because of the forgiving nature of the ingredients it also makes it the perfect totable dish: refrigerate or freeze it and then just pop it back into the oven to reheat. Whenever you need to bring comfort without a lot of fuss, this is the go-to recipe.

MAKES 4 TO 6 SERVINGS

FOR THE TOPPING

1½ pounds russet potatoes
(about 2 large potatoes)

3 tablespoons unsalted butter

¼ cup milk

1 egg yolk

1 teaspoon salt

FOR THE FILLING

2 tablespoons unsalted butter

1 chopped large yellow onion

1 cup peeled and chopped carrot

4 garlic cloves, minced

1 pound ground lamb (or beef if you prefer)

2 tablespoons all-purpose flour

1 cup beef broth

1 tablespoon Worcestershire sauce

¼ teaspoon ground cloves

1 teaspoon salt

1 teaspoon freshly ground black pepper

¾ cup peas (fresh or frozen work fine)

½ cup corn kernels (fresh or frozen work fine)

2 tablespoons chopped fresh parsley

2 tablespoons chopped fresh rosemary

Peel the potatoes and cut them into chunks. Put the potatoes in a large salted pot of water and bring to a boil. Cook for 10 to 15 minutes until the potatoes are completely tender. Drain the potatoes and then add them back into the empty pot with the butter, milk, egg yolk, and salt. Mash the potatoes until everything has combined but before it gets too smooth. It shouldn't be as creamy as your typical mashed potatoes: the thickness and lumpy texture helps the pie brown nicely on top. Set the potatoes aside.

Preheat the oven to 400°F.

Meanwhile, for the filling, heat a large skillet or pot on medium heat and add the butter. (If you like to serve in vessels that you cook in, such as a cast-iron pot, you can use that in this step and just use it for baking.) Once the butter has melted, add the onion and carrot and cook them until they start to brown slightly, approximately 3 or 4 minutes. Add the garlic cloves and lamb and allow it to brown another 3 to 4 minutes without stirring too much. Add the flour, broth, Worcestershire sauce, cloves, salt, and pepper and bring to a boil. Reduce the heat to low to simmer, and cook for 10 more minutes, until the filling is thick.

Turn the heat off and stir in the peas, corn, parsley, and rosemary. Taste to see if it needs more salt. Place the mixture in a baking dish and then spoon the mashed potatoes on top, spreading evenly.

Place in the oven on the middle rack and bake for 20 to 25 minutes, or until you see the mashed potatoes start to brown on top. If your oven doesn't tend to brown things evenly, you can turn the broiler on for the last minute to get a golden top. Remove from the oven and allow to cool at least 10 minutes before serving.

— HOW TO BRING IT —

This recipe does fine in the refrigerator or even the freezer. Make sure you let it all cool to room temperature before covering (the trapped steam will keep cooking the dish). Cover tightly and store it in the fridge for up to 3 days or in the freezer, well wrapped, for up to two months. To reheat, let the dish defrost in the fridge if frozen, and then cook for 20 minutes in a 350°F oven. You can also cook straight from frozen if you prefer, but it will change the texture a little bit.

Asparagus and Goat Cheese Tart

No matter who your audience is, this recipe will be a winner. My own vegetable-hating brother declared this one of his favorite recipes after initially being very skeptical. There's something about puff pastry that makes everyone happy. The combination of cheese and rosemary makes the asparagus more approachable to those less veggie inclined, and for those who live for vegetables, this dish is a delicious roasted treat.

MAKES 8 SERVINGS

12 ounces puff pastry dough

1 pound asparagus, ends trimmed

½ cup crumbled goat cheese

1 teaspoon salt

1 tablespoon rosemary, finely diced

¼ cup chopped spring onions (about 3 onions)

Preheat the oven to 350°F.

On a sheet pan lined with parchment paper (or lightly oiled if that is easier for you), spread out the puff pastry dough into a flat rectangle. Line up the asparagus spears side by side, leaving a bit of space on all the outer edges. Sprinkle the goat cheese, salt, rosemary, and spring onions on top. Fold the sides of the pastry dough over the asparagus (it shouldn't come so far as to cover more than one asparagus).

Place in the oven and cook for 30 to 40 minutes, or until you see the puff pastry browning and the asparagus has cooked.

— HOW TO BRING IT —

This dish can be served hot right out of the oven, or it can wait a whole day. If you are serving later, make sure to let it cool before wrapping in plastic wrap or aluminum foil so it does not continue to cook from trapped steam. Do not cut the tart until you are ready to serve.

Bacon Mushroom Quiche

You might think the secret to flavor is just adding bacon, but it's actually about layering. The bacon sings in this quiche, while the umami of the mushrooms and the extra layer of leek make it highly addictive. With eggs, the ultimate comfort food, as the base, you have a dish that will please any palate.

MAKES 6 TO 8 SERVINGS

1 pie crust (store bought or page 119)

1 tablespoon unsalted butter

3 slices bacon, diced

2 medium shallots, diced

1 cup sliced mushrooms

1 cup diced leeks (about 1 leek)

1 tablespoon fresh thyme

½ cup milk

5 eggs, beaten

1 teaspoon salt

¼ teaspoon freshly ground black pepper

¾ cup grated sharp Cheddar cheese, divided

Preheat the oven to 350°F.

Place the pie crust in a pie pan and crimp the edges. Bake for 5 to 7 minutes, until it has started to harden. Remove it from the oven and cool.

Meanwhile, place a pan on medium heat and melt the butter. Add the bacon, shallots, mushrooms, and leeks. Cook for 5 to 8 minutes until the bacon has begun to cook and the leeks have softened. Pour into a bowl and combine with the thyme, milk, eggs, salt, pepper, and ½ cup of the cheese.

Pour the mixture into the pie crust and sprinkle the remaining cheese on top. Bake for 35 to 45 minutes or until the quiche has set but is still slightly jiggly. Cool for at least 15 minutes before serving.

— HOW TO BRING IT —

Quiche can be served hot or cold. It takes well to reheating as long as the temperature in the oven is not over 350°F and you don't overcook it.

Broccoli and Almond Quiche

A party always needs a few vegetarian options, but that doesn't mean they have to be boring. This dish has everything you need from a quiche: texture, flavor, and a few ingredients that leave you guessing. The almonds are a particularly surprising addition, adding both flavor and crunch. You'll wonder why you hadn't thought of this combination before.

MAKES 8 SERVINGS

1 pie crust (store bought or page 119)

2 cups chopped broccoli

3 garlic cloves, diced

5 eggs, beaten

½ cup milk

½ cup slivered almonds

⅛ teaspoon cayenne

¼ teaspoon coriander

1 cup crumbled feta cheese

1 teaspoons salt

¼ teaspoon freshly ground black pepper

1 teaspoon parsley, finely diced

Preheat the oven to 350°F.

Place the pie crust in a pie pan and crimp the edges. Bake for 5 to 7 minutes, until it has started to harden. Remove it from the oven.

While the crust is baking, bring a pot of salted water to a boil. Blanch the broccoli for 3 minutes. Drain it in a colander, and rinse with cold water. Set aside and let the broccoli dry.

In a bowl combine the broccoli with the garlic, eggs, milk, almonds, cayenne, coriander, feta, salt, and pepper. Pour the mixture into the pie crust. Bake for 35 to 45 minutes or until the quiche has set but is still slightly jiggly (start checking on the early end of the range). Sprinkle the parsley on top and cool for at least 15 minutes before serving.

— HOW TO BRING IT —

Quiche can be served hot or cold. It reheats well at a low temp (under 350°F): don't overcook it or the eggs will be rubbery.

Cherry Tomato Tart

Sometimes you just want to bring the prettiest dish to the party. This tart will certainly succeed on that front, and the secret is that it's not that much work. If you get good-quality cherry tomatoes, this dish pretty much sells itself. Combining the acidity of the tomatoes with the umami of the cooked onions creates a light combination that is still surprisingly hearty.

MAKES 6 TO 8 SERVINGS

1 pie crust (store bought or page 119)

2 tablespoons butter

1 large onion, diced

3 garlic cloves, diced

1/2 cup shredded Parmesan cheese, divided

3 cups cherry tomatoes (or more if needed depending on size of tomatoes and crust)

1½ tablespoons fresh thyme

1 teaspoon salt

Preheat the oven to 450°F.

Place the pie crust in a pie pan and crimp the edges. Bake for 5 to 7 minutes, until it has started to harden. Remove it from the oven and cool.

Place a skillet on medium heat and melt the butter. Add the onion and garlic and cook for 10 to 15 minutes until the onions have browned. Add the onion mixture to the pie crust. Sprinkle ²/₃ of the Parmesan cheese on top of the pie crust and then add the cherry tomatoes on top. Make sure the cherry tomatoes really fill the pie: err on the side of overfilling rather than underfilling. They will settle as they bake. Sprinkle the thyme, the remaining Parmesan cheese, and the salt on top.

Place in the oven for 20 minutes or until the tomatoes start to brown and pop a little bit. Remove from the oven and cool before serving. Do note that this dish starts to fall apart once you begin cutting, so try to serve it all at once if possible.

— HOW TO BRING IT —

You can easily make this dish ahead of time, and it can be served piping hot, room temperature, or cold. It is easy to transport and doesn't need a lot of TLC on arrival, so it's a good one to bring somewhere where an oven isn't readily available. But as noted above, it's a bit crumbly so make sure it's left in a stable location with a good knife and an extra spoon to scoop.

Sausage, Tomato, and Kale Tart

This is a dish with a few ingredients that all come together sublimely. I love the comforting nature of a meat pie, and this dish is a lighter version. The tomatoes and kale keep it bright while the sausage adds depth, making it a true main course. Its seasonal versatility is also a plus: serve it in the winter for something hearty and warming, or serve it in the summer when the tomatoes are perfect.

MAKES 6 TO 8 SERVINGS

1 pie crust (store bought or page 119)

3 tablespoons unsalted butter

1 large white onion, diced

3 garlic cloves, minced

2 cups stemmed and chopped lacinato kale

8 ounces smoked link sausage

1½ cups chopped tomato

¼ cup chopped basil

1 egg, beaten

½ cup (4 ounces) goat cheese

1 teaspoon salt

¼ teaspoon freshly ground black pepper

Preheat the oven to 400°F.

Place the pie crust in a pie pan and crimp the edges. Bake for 5 to 7 minutes, until it has started to harden. Remove it from the oven and cool.

Meanwhile, place a large skillet on medium heat and melt the butter. Add the onion and garlic and cook 5 minutes until the onions start to brown. Add the kale and cook for 5 minutes, and then add the sausage and tomato and cook for an additional 3 minutes. Remove from the heat and allow it to cool for 5 minutes.

In a bowl combine the kale mixture with the basil, egg, goat cheese, salt, and pepper. Make sure the goat cheese is not clumping and pour into the crust. Bake the tart for 15 to 18 minutes in the oven, until the shell is browning and the filling is set. Cool and serve.

— HOW TO BRING IT —

You can serve this warm or at room temperature but try not to serve it completely chilled. You can make this a day ahead and reheat it in an oven: remove it from the fridge 30 minutes before and reheat at 350°F for 5 to 10 minutes. If you are planning to reheat, try to slightly undercook it the day before.

Pie Crust

Throughout the book there are quite a few recipes for pies and tarts. If you want to buy the crust, by all means do so. But if you are in the mood to make it, here is a recipe that will work for both savory and sweet dishes. It is based on my grandmother's recipe, which was all about keeping the dough as cool as possible. If you make that your goal, you can't go wrong.

MAKES 2 PIE CRUSTS

2½ cups all-purpose flour

1 teaspoon salt

2 tablespoons granulated sugar
(use 1½ teaspoons for savory dishes)

1 cup very cold unsalted butter (2 sticks),
chopped into small pieces

4 to 8 tablespoons ice-cold water

Stir together the flour, salt, and sugar. Add in the butter using two knives or a spoon, but try not to use your hands too much because you want the mixture to stay as cool as possible. You can also combine the dry ingredients with the butter in a food processor, using the pulse setting. The objective is to get the butter incorporated with the flour, creating pea-size pieces.

Slowly add in the water and mix until it just comes together as a dough. The amount varies depending on the type of flour and butter you use; it may take more or less liquid to bring together. Dump the dough out onto a sheet of plastic wrap, press together in a round, wrap well, and chill for at least an hour.

To roll out, flour a work surface well and divide the dough in half. Using a rolling pin (or an empty wine bottle if you don't have one), roll out each half into a ⅛-inch-thick round, creating two crusts. The crusts are now ready to be used.

CHAPTER 5

Meats and Fish

Every meal needs to have a main event.
But just because a dish is the center of attention
doesn't mean it should be overly complicated.
Main dishes at a shared meal should be easy to
serve, beautiful to look at, and impossible to resist
digging into for second helpings. But when you're
bringing proteins, you'll want to take a little extra
care: you can't let them sit out indefinitely, and you
also don't want to overcook. Finding the right
balance (and the right kinds of meats) is key.

Meats and Fish

———•———

RECIPES

Scallion Pesto Chicken

There's nothing like a whole roasted chicken, but for a group it's not the easiest item to serve. So instead go with the cut-up version. The bones add some extra flavor, and people can eat it with their hands. This dish does well at any temperature. Serve it piping hot for dinner or at room temperature for a picnic lunch.

MAKES 4 SERVINGS

2 cups chopped scallions
(about one small bunch)

6 tablespoons raw unsalted sunflower seeds

Juice of 2 lemons

6 garlic cloves

4 teaspoons capers

2 tablespoons extra-virgin olive oil

Dash of salt and freshly ground black pepper

1 whole chicken, cut into 8 pieces
(about 3 to 4 pounds)

Preheat the oven to 450°F.

Combine the scallions, sunflower seeds, lemon juice, garlic, capers, and oil in a blender and blend until there are no more lumps; divide between two bowls.

Lightly salt and pepper the chicken. Spread half of the scallion mixture on the chicken, reserving the second bowl, and then place the chicken on a foil-lined sheet pan, skin-side down. Put the chicken in the oven. After 15 minutes turn the chicken pieces over. After an additional 10 minutes, test the breast meat for doneness and remove it from the oven (unless it is much larger than the dark meat, it should be done). Let the dark meat cook for an additional 5 minutes, or until it reaches an internal temperature of 150°F (it will continue to rise to 160°F and then to 165°F as it rests). Spread the rest of the scallion sauce on top of the cooked chicken.

— HOW TO BRING IT —

You can serve this dish at room temperature, but if you would like to make it ahead, refrigerate, and reheat, just make sure to undercook it a bit so you don't dry it out. You can also serve the additional scallion sauce on the side if you'd like.

Chicken with Rosemary and Mustard

I am generally not a fan of dishes made with boneless, skinless chicken breasts. Skin and bones add depth and flavor; without them, chicken breasts tend to be a little drier than I would like. Still, I cannot argue with the ease and crowd-pleasing factors that chicken breasts afford, especially if you are serving a big group. To make everyone happy, I found my own little compromise: I brine the chicken breasts before cooking to ensure that the meat is moist. I know the word "brine" brings up a time-consuming nightmare of raw meat submerged for hours on end, but with chicken breasts, it's super quick and easy: even 15 minutes of brining will vastly improve your chicken. Then to top it all off, I add a flavorful sauce to give the chicken the punch it needs. If you were ever a chicken breast skeptic, this might be the recipe that converts you.

MAKES 4 TO 8 SERVINGS

¼ cup salt plus additional for seasoning, divided

4 cups warm water

4 pounds large boneless skinless chicken breast halves (each breast should be at least ½ pound to hold up well to brining; see note)

4 tablespoons Dijon mustard

2 tablespoons extra-virgin olive oil

1½ tablespoons very finely chopped rosemary

3 garlic cloves, minced

2 tablespoons fresh lemon juice (about ½ a lemon)

Stir the ¼ cup of salt into the warm water until the salt has dissolved, and then chill the brine completely. Place the chicken breasts in a large shallow baking dish and pour the brine carefully over the top. Cover and refrigerate for 1 hour, turning halfway through. You can brine for less time if needed but try not to go much past 1 hour as the brine starts to change the texture of the meat.

Combine the mustard, oil, rosemary, garlic, and lemon juice in a bowl. Once the meat is brined, remove it from the liquid and pat dry with paper towels. Coat the chicken breasts with the mustard mixture and then sprinkle salt on both sides.

Place a grill pan or regular frying pan over medium-high heat. Once the pan is hot, cook the chicken breasts in batches for 4 to 8 minutes on each side: depending on the size of your chicken breasts, size and cooking time can vary widely. Be careful not to move the breasts too much so that they develop a brown crust. You'll know when the meat is done when the internal temperature reaches 150°F; the meat will continue to cook a bit more from residual heat as it sits, getting up to 160°F to 165°F. You can also do the touch test: if you touch a breast in the center and it feels firm without giving too much, then it's done. Remove the chicken from the heat and let it rest at least 5 minutes before serving.

NOTE: If you decide to use chicken breasts smaller than ½ pound, you may not use all of the mustard sauce and your brining and cooking times will be less.

— HOW TO BRING IT —

Cold chicken is still delightful, so if you want to serve it cold or at room temperature that will work as well. If you are serving for a group, you can cut it into slices. Just make sure to let it rest at least 5 minutes before cutting into it. If you want to serve this hot, undercook the chicken a bit and refrigerate immediately, then let it come back to room temperature before cooking again. Reheat it over medium-high heat to finish it off.

Vinegar Chicken with Tomatoes

This is a variation on a dish I once learned from the famed French chef Daniel Boulud: he was showcasing a recipe his mother made for him when he was growing up. Its homespun flavor could have gone toe to toe with any of the fancier dishes in his restaurant. The secret is the vinegar and tarragon. These two ingredients combine to reinvigorate chicken. This version is easier than Daniel's but no less full of joie de vivre.

MAKES 4 SERVINGS

2 tablespoons unsalted butter

4 shallots, diced

1 whole chicken, cut into 6 or 8 pieces (about 3 pounds)

Salt and freshly ground black pepper

2 garlic cloves, diced

½ cup red wine vinegar

¼ cup chopped tarragon

1 cup chicken stock

2 cups halved cherry tomatoes, divided

1 cup diced tomatoes, any medium or large variety

In a large Dutch oven or braising pan, melt the butter over medium-high heat. Add the shallots and cook for 2 minutes, stirring consistently.

Season the chicken evenly with salt and pepper. Add the chicken to the pan in batches and cook approximately 4 to 7 minutes on each side, or until the skin is golden. Add the garlic, vinegar, tarragon, and chicken stock to the chicken. Allow the liquid to heat to a simmer while scraping the bottom of the pan. Add half of the cherry tomatoes and all of the diced tomatoes to the pan and cover. Reduce the heat to medium low and cook for an additional 10 minutes.

If the smaller pieces of chicken are already cooked, you can remove them here. Add the remaining tomatoes and cover and cook for another 10 minutes, or until the chicken is cooked through. Remove the rest of the chicken and cook down the sauce on high heat for approximately 10 to 15 minutes until it reduces to a thicker consistency, stirring frequently so it doesn't burn. Return the chicken to the pan and serve hot.

— HOW TO BRING IT —

This dish can be made ahead: undercook the chicken by 10 minutes and then bring to room temperature and refrigerate, covered. You can then reheat over low heat for 10 minutes before serving. You can serve this dish at room temperature, but it is best when hot.

Tahini Lamb and Rice

This dish is great for a few reasons: you will look fancy if you serve lamb, but by using the stewing meat it won't break the bank. And this one-pot wonder really brings the flavor. It's the kind of sauce that intrigues and excites without any one flavor in particular overpowering it. My sister hates cumin and usually dislikes any dish that has it, but she didn't even notice I had sneaked it in because everything blended together so perfectly. Don't let the long cooking time deter you. It's worth it.

MAKES 6 SERVINGS

2 tablespoons extra-virgin olive oil

2 pounds lamb stewing meat, cubed (shoulder or leg, whichever is easiest to find)

4 garlic cloves, diced

1 white onion, diced

1 cup dry white wine, divided

1 teaspoon cumin

1 teaspoon coriander

¼ cup plus 1 tablespoon tahini, divided

Juice of 2 lemons, divided

¼ cup chopped flat leaf parsley

¼ cup Greek yogurt

1½ cups white rice

1 cup quartered cherry tomatoes

2 teaspoons salt

Set a Dutch oven (or other large pot with a lid) on medium heat. Add the olive oil and then the lamb in batches, browning each side, approximately 1 minute on each side, no more than 5 minutes total. Add the garlic, onion, and ¼ cup of the white wine to the pot: use the liquid to scrape up any brown bits from the bottom. Cook for 5 minutes or until the onion starts to brown. Add the remaining wine, 1 cup water, cumin, coriander, 1 tablespoon of the tahini, and the juice of 1 lemon. Reduce heat, cover, and cook for 2 hours or until the meat starts to fall apart when poked. Stir every 30 minutes or so. If at any point the liquid level looks too low, you can add ½ cup of water—just make sure that by the end you have more of a sauce than a soup.

While the lamb is cooking, in a bowl combine the remaining ¼ cup tahini, juice of the remaining lemon, parsley, and Greek yogurt. Set aside.

Make the rice: bring 2 cups of water to a boil. Add the white rice and cook for 15 to 20 minutes until the water is absorbed. It should be cooked but slightly al dente: you can add more or less water depending on your brand of rice. Set it aside until the lamb finishes cooking.

When the lamb is finished cooking, remove from the heat, add the cherry tomatoes, salt, and cooked rice to the mixture. Pour the tahini mixture on top and serve.

— HOW TO BRING IT —

If you make this dish ahead of time, just be sure to bring it back up to temperature when serving. Place it back on the stove for a minute or two to heat through, stirring occasionally. You could also put it in a 350°F oven for 5 to 10 minutes (depending on how cold it was to begin with), also stirring. You can add the juice from an extra half a lemon to perk it up if needed.

Ginger Beef

Any time you serve meat at room temperature, you need a sauce that makes people forget they could've eaten something right out of the oven. With only a few major ingredients, this sauce gets the job done. You can use this sauce on a lot of different proteins (I've yet to find something that doesn't go with it), but it marries particularly well with steak. The bold, bright sauce perfectly complements the robust nature of beef. After all, who could ever argue with steak?

MAKES 4 TO 8 SERVINGS

1/3 cup finely chopped fresh ginger

2 cups finely chopped scallions

2 tablespoons soy sauce

1 teaspoon balsamic vinegar

1 tablespoon extra-virgin olive oil

Dash of salt

4 pounds sirloin steak

1/4 cup vegetable or canola oil

Make the sauce: Combine the ginger, scallions, soy sauce, vinegar, and olive oil. Set it aside. (I think the sauce gets better the longer it sits, but at least let it sit while you cook the steak so it has time to settle together.)

Then make the steaks: Generously salt the steaks on both sides. Place a cast-iron or nonstick pan on very high heat and add the oil (only use half if you are making the steaks in two batches to keep from crowding the pan). Let the oil get hot and cook each steak for 5 to 8 minutes, depending on the size of your steaks and the desired level of doneness. You will want to flip each steak every 30 seconds or so to ensure that it cooks evenly: it will cook better this way rather than flipping it only once—I promise.

Remove the steaks and let them rest for at least 5 minutes. Slice off the fat and cut the steaks lengthwise into 1/4-inch-wide strips. Add the sauce on top and serve.

— HOW TO BRING IT —

This dish is great hot or cold. If you are serving it cold, you can keep both the sauce and the cooked meat in the fridge for a day before serving (the sauce can keep for 3 days). If you are going to refrigerate the meat for later, don't slice it after cooking: wait until you are about to serve it so the moisture in the meat stays intact. If you want to serve the meat hot, undercook it a bit when making it and then reheat it from room temperature in an oven at 350°F for a few minutes to get it up to temperature. You can microwave the sauce to get it hot if you like.

Short Ribs with Quick Pickled Shallots

My sister's birthday is in February, and this has become my go-to dish to celebrate. It is full of so much flavor that it can warm even the frostiest of days. It can be served hot from a single pan, or you can store it and reheat it. Short ribs are tough to mess up, and they will serve you well as long as you give them enough flavor to absorb. And that flavor is the key. To balance out the richness of the dish, we have a secret weapon: pickled shallots. I know the word "pickled" can spark fear but don't let it: simply let the shallots sit while the ribs cook. They're an easy addition that makes a world of difference. This dish will improve with age, so make ahead if you can: a day in the fridge will make it more flavorful. It's a complete win-win.

MAKES 4 TO 6 SERVINGS

FOR THE SHORT RIBS

5 to 6 pounds of bone-in short ribs

Salt and freshly ground black pepper, plus extra salt for seasoning

1 tablespoon vegetable oil

2 large carrots, diced

1 large onion, diced

2 cups diced mushrooms (about 1 pound)

4 garlic cloves, minced

2 cups red wine

1 tablespoon Dijon mustard

2 teaspoons Worcestershire sauce

1 tablespoon tomato paste

2 cups beef stock

1 tablespoon thyme

1 tablespoon chopped rosemary

FOR THE PICKLED SHALLOTS

½ cup apple cider vinegar

1 tablespoon granulated sugar

2 teaspoons salt

4 shallots, diced

Preheat the oven to 350°F.

Sprinkle salt and pepper on the ribs. Set a large pot on medium heat and add the oil (I like to use a cast-iron Dutch oven here if possible). Once the oil is hot, add the ribs and sear them in batches on each side for 2 to 3 minutes, until they have started to brown.

Set the cooked ribs aside and then add the carrots, onion, and mushrooms. Cook for 5 minutes, stirring, then add the garlic and cook another 2 minutes, or until the vegetables have begun to soften. Add the red wine to deglaze the pan, scraping the brown bits off the bottom of the pan, and bring to a boil. Cook for an additional 10 minutes or until the liquid has reduced by half, stirring occasionally.

Add the mustard, Worcestershire sauce, tomato paste, stock, thyme, rosemary, and salt and stir together. Go easy on the salt, since the liquid will reduce (you can always add more but you can't take it away). Add the ribs back into the pot, bring the liquid back up to a boil, and cover tightly.

Place in the oven and cook for 3 hours or until the ribs are tender. If your pot is fairly full, you may want to put a pan lined with aluminum foil on the rack underneath the pot in case there is any spillage.

While the ribs are cooking, make the shallots. Whisk the cider vinegar, sugar, and salt together until everything has dissolved. Add the shallots and let them sit at room temperature while the ribs are cooking for at least 3 hours and up to 5, and then drain the shallots, rinse them, and set aside.

Once the ribs are finished remove the pot from the oven.

To serve immediately, skim as much fat off the top as possible (there will be a lot). The sauce should be a pretty soupy consistency, so remove the ribs and cook down the sauce on medium-high heat for 10 to 15 minutes until the sauce has reduced, stirring frequently. Add the ribs back into the pot and taste: add more salt here if needed. Sprinkle the pickled shallots on top and serve.

— HOW TO BRING IT —

One of the joys of this dish is that it actually gets *better* if you bring it. The longer it sits, the more the flavors develop. To make it ahead, allow it to cool down for 30 minutes after removing it from the oven and then refrigerate. It can stay in the fridge for up to 2 days. When you are ready to serve, spoon off the fat: it will have congealed and will be easy to remove. Reheat in a 350°F oven for 15 minutes and then move to the stovetop and remove the ribs. Cook down the sauce on medium-high heat for 10 to 15 minutes until the sauce has reduced, stirring frequently. Add the ribs back into the pot and taste: add more salt here if needed. Sprinkle the pickled shallots on top and serve.

Another suggestion for bringing this dish is to remove the bones from the ribs ahead of time. If people are eating standing up, or if they are likely to have a lot on their plates, removing the bones will make the dish easier to eat. Remove the meat from the bones and return it into the sauce. The dish won't have the same presentation value but it will be much easier to serve and eat.

Hoppin' John

Hoppin' John, a classic Southern dish, is served on New Year's Day and is supposed to bring good luck. There are all sorts of myths about why it is lucky, but I think the real reason must be that it's so delicious that the person who makes it always comes out looking like an excellent cook. You can serve it as a hearty, rice bowl main or as a side if you prefer. Purists will have a lot to say about my version, and that's okay. Many call for fresh peas. Many say to cook the rice separately. I say make a delicious dish simple and you will make it more often.

MAKES 6 SERVINGS

1 tablespoon extra-virgin olive oil

4 ounces bacon, cut into ¼-inch cubes

3 garlic cloves, minced

1 large onion, chopped

2 tablespoons fresh thyme leaves
(fresh preferred, but substitute
1 tablespoon dried)

2 cups diced fresh tomatoes, divided

1⅓ cups chicken stock

1 cup white or basmati rice

1 (14- to 16-ounce) can black-eyed peas,
drained and rinsed

Dash of salt and freshly ground
black pepper

Dash of red pepper flakes (optional)

Place a large saucepan over medium-high heat and add the olive oil, bacon, garlic, and onion. Cook for 5 to 7 minutes, stirring occasionally until the onions start to look translucent. Add the thyme, 1 cup of the tomatoes, and the chicken stock. Bring to a boil and add the rice. Mix together, cover, and reduce the heat to low. Cook for 12 to 13 minutes or until the rice is almost done. Depending on the type of rice you use, this can vary widely so look at the packaging. Add the black-eyed peas, remaining tomatoes, salt and pepper to taste, and red pepper flakes if you like them. Cook an additional 2 minutes and then serve.

— HOW TO BRING IT —

If you need to make this ahead of time, leave everything a little undercooked: reserve the last 1/3 cup of chicken stock, only cook it for 10 minutes, and only add the final ingredients once it has cooled down. Once you arrive, you can put it back on a stove with the remaining chicken stock for a few minutes and get it all back up to temperature. This dish is at its best hot or warm.

— SUBSTITUTIONS —

It feels blasphemous to say this, but you *can* make this dish vegetarian if you need to. You can use vegetable stock and the bean liquid in place of the chicken stock and exclude the bacon—but keep in mind the dish will be much less flavorful though still delicious. Try to include the red pepper flakes because a bit of spice will add some flavor back in.

Spice-Crusted Pork

Pork tenderloin is a great meat at any temperature, but because it is lean I like to spice it up a bit—and this recipe definitely brings the spice. It's not too hot (for those who are fearful), but it has a nice kick and a lot of flavor. This version adds yogurt as a coating instead of oil because it adds a bit of tang as well as protecting the meat from drying out. It's a main dish that feels complex in taste without being particularly hard to make: the perfect combination.

MAKES 4 TO 6 SERVINGS

3 tablespoons Greek yogurt

1 tablespoon Dijon mustard

1 tablespoon fresh lemon juice

1 teaspoon garlic powder

½ teaspoon cayenne

2 teaspoons salt

1 teaspoon freshly ground black pepper

2 teaspoons ground coriander

2 teaspoons herbes de Provence

2 pounds pork tenderloin

1 tablespoon extra-virgin olive oil

Preheat the oven to 400°F.

Combine the yogurt, mustard, and lemon juice in one bowl. In another bowl, combine the garlic powder, cayenne, salt, pepper, coriander, and herbes de Provence. Coat the pork tenderloin in the yogurt mixture and then liberally sprinkle the spice mixture on top. Make sure the spices completely cover the tenderloin all the way around.

Place a wide oven-safe pan or skillet on a stovetop burner on medium-high heat and add in the olive oil. Once the pan is hot, put the pork tenderloin in and cook for 6 minutes, turning to ensure that there is browning on all sides. Transfer the skillet to the oven, and cook for an additional 15 minutes, or until it reaches 135°F to 140°F, depending on how rare you like it. Remember, it will continue cooking even after removed from the oven.

Remove from the oven and wait at least 3 minutes before carving the tenderloin.

— HOW TO BRING IT —

This dish can be made a day ahead and then served at room temperature. You don't want it to be completely cold, so just make sure you remove it from the refrigerator at least 30 minutes before serving. Don't slice the meat before you are ready to serve it. Wrap it in aluminum foil (after it is done cooling), refrigerate it for up to a day, and then only carve once you are ready to go. That way it will retain its moisture. If you insist on reheating it, just be sure to undercook it a bit the day before so it doesn't overcook: tough pork tenderloin is no one's idea of fun.

Roasted Watermelon Pork Ribs

One of my favorite chefs, Floyd Cardoz, makes a dish that uses watermelon as a sauce for fish. When I first ate it, the whole concept delighted me: the little bit of sweet balanced out and complemented the savory. I have always loved watermelon with barbecue, so the fish dish inspired me to take the concept and flip it around with pork. It is unexpected but works so perfectly you'll wonder why you weren't making a watermelon sauce before.

MAKES 6 TO 8 SERVINGS

6 cups (roughly 2 pounds) seedless watermelon

2 cups cider vinegar

2 teaspoons honey

3 racks of baby back ribs (about 5 pounds)

Salt and freshly ground black pepper

Blend the watermelon in a blender until there are no chunks left. Add the watermelon to a wide pot with the vinegar and bring it up to a boil. Let the purée reduce for 20 to 30 minutes until it has reached a thick ketch-up-like consistency. The timing will depend on the size of your pot: if you want to speed it up, try using a Dutch oven or a large, wide skillet. Add in the honey and stir.

While the sauce is reducing, turn on your broiler. Salt the ribs generously on both sides and place on a wire rack on top of a sheet pan. Put the ribs in the oven under the broiler for 5 to 7 minutes, with the meat side up. Remove once the meat has started to brown and let cool. Reduce the temperature to 300°F.

Take the ribs off the rack and set them on a few large sheets of aluminum foil: you're going to wrap the ribs tightly so be generous with the foil. Brush the watermelon sauce on top of the ribs, add another sprinkling of salt and some pepper, and then wrap the ribs in the aluminum foil. Be careful to wrap them well and with a few layers: if the juices start leaking out you can end up with a lot of burned sauce in your pan.

Place the wrapped ribs on a sheet pan and put in the oven. Cook them for 2½ to 3 hours (depending on their size and how tender you like them). Remove from the oven, unwrap, and serve.

— HOW TO BRING IT —

I love cold ribs. and these are easily served cold or at room temperature. They can be made a day or two ahead; just store them in the aluminum foil until you are ready to serve them.

If you make them ahead and want to serve them hot, you have a couple of options. You can broil the ribs, let cool, and then brush with sauce and wrap in foil, cooking them only before you want to eat. They are easily transported in their foil, still hot. Another alternative is to fully cook them and then reheat them once you arrive. Ribs are very forgiving so you can heat them up without worrying about overcooking them. The biggest thing is not to remove them from the aluminum foil: you never want to lose the sauce, so try to keep it inside until ready to serve, whatever the scenario.

Paprika Shrimp

I used to go shrimping a lot as a kid, and shrimp have always been one of my favorites. Yet they are so easy to get wrong: overcooking is usually their undoing. This recipe is all about cooking them right and with the right sauce. You don't want too much sauce, or the result is something too soupy that hides the flavor, but you want enough zing to make them exciting. This accomplishes both. I have two requests to make before you start. Please try not to buy farmed shrimp if you can—the shrimp don't taste half as good and industrial shrimp farms are among the worst polluters in the world. And please buy plenty of shrimp—don't skimp on quantity. I know these two directives are likely in conflict with your grocery budget, but this is a splurge kind of recipe. I promise you won't be sorry!

MAKES 4 TO 6 SERVINGS

1 teaspoon paprika

1/2 teaspoon Sriracha

1 teaspoon balsamic vinegar

1 teaspoon extra-virgin olive oil

2 teaspoons salt

2 pounds peeled and deveined shrimp

1 cup scallions, diced (about 6 to 8 scallions), plus a few teaspoons to sprinkle

1 (14-ounce) can cannellini beans, drained

Combine the paprika, Sriracha, balsamic vinegar, olive oil, and salt in a large bowl. Add the shrimp, scallions, and beans and toss until everything is coated.

Place a skillet on very high heat. Once the pan is very hot, add the shrimp mixture and let the shrimp cook for 2 to 3 minutes on each side: be careful not to stir too much since you are aiming to brown the shrimp. Remove from the heat, sprinkle on the additional scallions, and serve.

— HOW TO BRING IT —

This dish is quick to cook, so you can prep it and keep it in the fridge for up to 12 hours if needed. If you are serving it cold or at room temperature, remove the shrimp from the heat and let it cool down before putting it into a container: the shrimp will keep cooking from the steam if you cover it when hot. If you are going to reheat it on arrival, be sure to undercook a bit; reheat in a pan or in the oven carefully before serving.

Also note that this is a 30 minutes or less recipe, but only if you buy the shrimp pre-peeled. If not, add some extra time into your equation.

Sausage Jambalaya

I love when just the sound of a word describes a dish completely. Jambalaya has that effect for me. It sounds like a bunch of comforting deliciousness made in a single pot, and that's essentially what it is. Jambalaya is a New Orleans–inspired dish that just needs some rice, a meat or seafood, and a bit of Cajun spice to qualify. This version is made with totability in mind because sausage is the ultimate food for reheating and serving to groups. With other jambalayas that call for shrimp or chicken, it can dry out easily, but here we double down on sausages, using different kinds to bring different textural and flavor dimensions. On top of that, unlike stews and other Cajun flavors, you can put this dish together fairly quickly. Flavorful, comforting, and fast—the perfect meal.

MAKES 6 TO 8 SERVINGS

1 tablespoon vegetable oil

1 green bell pepper, thinly diced

1 celery stalk, thinly chopped

1 medium onion, chopped

4 garlic cloves, diced

1 pound sweet Italian pork sausage

8 ounces fresh chorizo

1 (28-ounce) can diced tomatoes

2 cups long grain white rice

2 cups chicken broth

1/4 teaspoon cayenne

1/4 teaspoon paprika (smoked if you have it, but any variety will do)

Juice of 1 lemon, divided

Salt to taste

3 scallions, sliced

8 ounces salami, chopped into very small pieces

Heat the oil on medium-high heat in a large heavy pot like a Dutch oven. Add the pepper, celery, and onion and cook until the vegetables start to soften, about 5 minutes. Add the garlic, sausage, and chorizo and cook an additional 3 minutes (try not to stir too much so the sausage browns a bit). Add the tomatoes, rice, broth, cayenne, paprika, and half the lemon juice. Bring the liquid to a boil. Reduce the heat, cover tightly, and cook until the liquid is absorbed, approximately 20 to 25 minutes. Cooking time will heavily depend on the brand of rice, so follow the package instructions. You can stir occasionally but try not to lift the lid too much, especially in the first 10 minutes, to keep the moisture inside.

When the liquid has been absorbed, salt to taste—the sausage, stock, and tomatoes may add plenty, so be sure to taste. Stir in the scallions, the rest of the lemon juice, and the salami.

— HOW TO BRING IT —

You can make jambalaya a day ahead. Let it cool down completely before covering and refrigerating. To reheat, add a bit of water and set it on low heat, stirring frequently until it comes back up to temperature.

— SUBSTITUTIONS —

The types of sausage here can be interchangeable. One should be a bit spicier or more flavorful, and then a hard sausage to add in at the end.

Sweet and Sour Fish

Some flavors are so outstanding that people will think you did something extra special when really all you did was rub on a single ingredient. Tamarind is that kind of ingredient. It is distinctive without being alienating and tart enough to bring anything to life. If your local grocery store doesn't carry it, don't worry: tamarind is shelf stable, which means you can easily order it online. Once you try it on this fish, you'll find yourself slapping tamarind on everything.

MAKES 6 SERVINGS

1½ tablespoons tamarind paste

3 garlic cloves, finely chopped or grated

1 teaspoon salt

2 limes, divided

1 tablespoon extra-virgin olive oil

6 red snapper fillets or another meaty white fish (6 ounces each)

2 tablespoons chopped parsley

Preheat the oven to 350°F and line a sheet pan with aluminum foil.

Whisk together the tamarind paste, garlic, salt, and the juice of half a lime. Spread the olive oil on both sides of the snapper fillets and place them skin-side down on the sheet pan. Brush the tamarind mixture evenly across the top of the fillets.

Place them in the oven for 8 to 10 minutes, depending on the thickness of your fillets. Slice your remaining limes into quarters. Remove the snapper fillets from the oven and sprinkle parsley on top. Serve with a lime wedge next to each piece of snapper.

— HOW TO BRING IT —

This versatile dish can be served hot or at room temperature. You can make the fish a day in advance and serve it at room temperature, but wait until you are serving it to sprinkle the parsley on top.

Seafood Paella-ish

Paella is one of those dishes so steeped in tradition that a lot of purists start crying foul whenever you even mention deviating from the rules. But finding Spanish rice and buying a paella pan isn't possible for everyone, so let's say this dish was inspired by paella, and we can accept that it will be a bit easier than the original. In a traditional seafood paella, you'd have a lot of shellfish on top for a pretty presentation, but to make this dish more portable we have opted to keep it light. The shrimp is pre-peeled, and there are no clamshells sticking awkwardly on the side of a plate. This dish has bold flavors without all the hassle. It might not be traditional, but it is delectable.

MAKES 4 TO 6 SERVINGS

3 tablespoons extra-virgin olive oil

4 garlic cloves, diced

1 large onion, diced

1 cup chopped tomato

1 teaspoon paprika

1/2 teaspoon saffron threads

1/4 teaspoon cayenne

1 cup dry white wine

2 1/2 cups chicken broth or fish stock

Dash of salt, divided

1 pound squid, cut the body into 1/4-inch rings, keep the tentacles whole

2 cups Spanish paella rice or arborio or carnaroli rice

1/2 cup chopped flat leaf parsley, divided

1/2 cup chopped scallions

1 red bell pepper, deseeded and diced

Juice of 2 lemons, divided

2 tablespoons sherry vinegar

8 ounces thick white fish such as cod

1 pound peeled shrimp

1 cup frozen peas

Put a wide rimmed pan, like a Dutch oven or a paella pan if you have one, on the stove over medium heat; add the olive oil, then the garlic, onion, tomato, paprika, saffron, and cayenne. Cook for about 10 minutes until the tomato starts to break down and become a bit jam-like.

In a separate pot bring the wine and broth to a boil, and add a dash of salt if the broth is not already salted.

Add the squid to the rimmed pan and cook for 1 minute. Next, add the rice, 1/4 cup of the parsley, the scallions, the red pepper, the juice of 1 1/2 lemons, and the sherry vinegar. Stir together until the rice is completely coated. Add the wine and broth mixture to the pan and stir. Make sure the rice is spread completely evenly across the pan and that the heat is on medium or medium low to keep the liquid at a low simmer throughout. If it isn't simmering, turn the heat up a bit. Cook for 12 minutes, turning the pan without stirring every 3 or 4 minutes to ensure that the rice is cooking evenly.

Cut the cod into 1-inch pieces and lightly salt it and the shrimp. Add the cod, shrimp, and peas to the pan and spread them evenly on

(recipe continues)

top of the rice. Be careful not to stir the rice: you want to make sure you have some crust on the bottom. Cover the pan. If your pot has a lid then use that, if not use foil. Cook for an additional 10 minutes or until the shrimp and cod are cooked and the rice has absorbed the broth. Uncover, and sprinkle the remaining parsley on top with the remaining lemon juice. Add more salt as needed.

NOTE: The kind of rice you are using can dramatically alter the timing of this dish, so read the package instructions. You certainly can stir, but try not to until the end: you want to get that delicious crust on the bottom of the pan, which you can then scrape into the rice. However, if your rice doesn't seem to be absorbing the liquid as quickly as you'd like, it's okay to stir it a little and take more time. Taste as you go along, and make sure to taste at the end to see if you need a bit more salt.

— HOW TO BRING IT —

If you are serving this dish to a big group, make sure the fish and shrimp are *just* cooked since they will sit for a while. You can travel with this dish but you should only cook the seafood for 3 to 4 minutes initially and then reheat the dish on arrival. You can heat it on the stovetop or pop it into a 350°F oven, covered, for 5 to 10 minutes. In either case, try to heat it from room temperature rather than cold; otherwise, you'll overcook the seafood.

— SUBSTITUTIONS —

This dish can have many variations depending on what seafood you have available. Almost any seafood can work, just be aware of cooking times.

Cold Dill Salmon

Cold salmon can make you think of bad buffets, but this poaching method changes the game. The goal is to keep the salmon moist and flavorful despite its time in the fridge. And instead of worrying about traveling around with a hot dish, you'll have a dish that is perfectly content to be cold. It's as easy to make as it is to serve.

MAKES 4 SERVINGS

1 medium-size shallot

¼ cup dill plus extra to garnish

2 tablespoons fresh lemon juice, divided (about ½ a lemon)

½ teaspoon coriander

1 garlic clove

¼ cup full fat plain yogurt

1 cup dry white wine

4 salmon fillets (6 to 8 ounces each)

Dash of salt

Add the shallot, dill, half of the lemon juice, coriander, and garlic to a blender and blend until combined. Stir in the yogurt and set aside.

Put 3 cups of water, the wine, and remaining lemon juice in a saucepan or large skillet, cover, and bring to a simmer just before a boil. Add the fish and lower the heat to maintain a low simmer and cover. There should be enough liquid to fully submerge the fish. If it isn't quite deep enough, just add more wine and water in the same ratio. Simmer until the salmon is just starting to look cooked, the outside turning a bit white, about 4 to 5 minutes; cooking time will vary depending on the thickness of the salmon.

Turn off the heat and let the fish stand in the liquid for an additional 2 to 3 minutes, covered. Remove the salmon from the liquid and refrigerate. Once the salmon is cold, sprinkle salt over the fish and spread the yogurt mixture over the top. Finish with a garnish of fresh dill. Bring the fish to room temperature for at least 30 minutes before serving.

— HOW TO BRING IT —

You can make this dish a day ahead, but store the fish and yogurt sauce separately.

Soy-Glazed Mackerel

Mackerel really doesn't get enough respect. Because it is an oily fish with a pronounced flavor, some people write it off as too fishy. But that's missing the beauty of mackerel: it's a sustainable fish that also happens to be cheap—something that we rarely see together—and to top it all off, its oiliness means it is much harder to overcook than a lot of other fish. The type of mackerel will influence the cooking time: thicker Spanish mackerel should take a bit longer than the thinner American varieties. If you're looking for a fish to stand up and hold on, mackerel is your match. What it really needs is a good sauce to make it sing, and that's what this recipe is for. It is simple, full of flavor, and ready to change your mind about mackerel.

MAKES 6 SERVINGS

⅓ cup soy sauce

⅓ cup sherry vinegar

¼ cup maple syrup

6 mackerel fillets (6 to 8 ounces each), with skin on

Dash of salt and freshly ground black pepper

Combine the soy sauce, vinegar, and maple syrup in a small saucepan on medium-high heat. Bring to a boil and then reduce the heat so that the mixture is simmering. Stir occasionally until the sauce begins to reduce, about 20 minutes. Remove the sauce from the heat.

Turn on the broiler in the oven and line a sheet pan with aluminum foil. Brush the sauce on both sides of the mackerel fillets. Place them skin-side down on the pan, and cook under the broiler for 3 to 5 minutes: the timing depends on the type and thickness of mackerel. The fillets should just start to firm up.

Remove the fillets, brush more glaze on both sides, and place them back in the oven skin side up for another 2 minutes until the fish is cooked through: the fillets should be slightly opaque in the center—a whiter color than their raw, more translucent state. During the second phase of cooking, keep a close eye on the fish: because of the oily nature of the skin, it should start to char. You won't eat the skin, but the char adds depth to the flavor. Just make sure to pull the fillets out before the skin chars too much. Add a dash of salt and pepper to the tops of the fillets before serving.

— HOW TO BRING IT —

This recipe is great hot: you can make the glaze in advance and then broil the fish upon arrival in less than 10 minutes. However, it does well at room temperature because of the powerful flavor of the sauce. You can make it in the morning and refrigerate it for up to 12 hours before serving. Remove it for at least 15 to 30 minutes before serving so it can begin to come back to room temperature.

— SUBSTITUTIONS —

If you can't find sherry vinegar, you can use balsamic vinegar instead.

Mustard Salmon

Because of salmon's firm texture and pronounced flavor, it works served cold, hot, or at room temperature. Mustard adds in well here because its tangy nature matches up with the salmon, and it, like salmon, is good either cold or hot. The addition of mayonnaise might feel out of place, but it will help to keep the salmon moist. It's a simple dish that looks more impressive than it actually is—key to any totable dish.

MAKES 6 SERVINGS

2 tablespoons mayonnaise

1 tablespoon Dijon mustard

1 teaspoon salt

2 pounds whole salmon fillet

1 tablespoon extra-virgin olive oil

1 tablespoon whole grain mustard

1 tablespoon fresh lime juice

1 teaspoon grated lime zest

1 tablespoon sliced chives

Preheat the oven to 350°F.

Combine the mayonnaise, Dijon mustard, and salt. Brush the salmon with olive oil and place on a sheet pan. Spread the mustard sauce evenly over the salmon. Roast in the oven for 12 minutes; however, depending on the thickness of your salmon, you might want a few minutes more or less. Remove from the oven.

Combine the whole grain mustard and the lime juice. Spread the lime mixture on top of the salmon and then sprinkle the lime zest and chives on top. Serve hot or refrigerate and serve later at room temperature.

— HOW TO BRING IT —

This dish can be made a day in advance as long as you are planning to serve it cold or at room temperature. You don't want to reheat something that has such a short cooking time. To store it, make sure to let it fully cool to room temperature and then wrap it tightly and refrigerate. If you are traveling with this dish, you may want to hold off adding the lime zest and chives until you arrive so that it all looks fresh.

Spicy Whole Fish with Cilantro and Peppers

There is something about a whole fish that elevates the presentation. You certainly can do this recipe with fillets (the cooking time is pretty much the same), but keeping it whole will make everything look nicer. Any thick white fish will work well: find whatever is fresh at your fish counter and use this recipe to complement it. This recipe seems to have a lot of parts, but it is simple to make and it all melds beautifully together. There's a bit of spice, a bit of heat, and a lot of flavor.

MAKES 6 SERVINGS

¼ cup chopped cilantro, plus extra for garnish

¼ cup chopped fresh parsley

4 garlic cloves

1 teaspoon cumin

1 small jalapeño pepper, seeded

2 tablespoons white wine

1 tablespoon soy sauce

1 tablespoon grated ginger

Juice of 1 lemon

2 red or yellow bell peppers

2½ to 3 pounds of a white fish like snapper or grouper

Dash of salt and freshly ground black pepper

Preheat the oven to 475°F. Put the cilantro, parsley, garlic, cumin, jalapeño, white wine, soy sauce, ginger, and lemon juice in a blender and blend until it forms a uniform sauce.

Halve the peppers, remove the seeds, and cut them into strips. Toss the peppers in the sauce and then spread the sauce and peppers evenly on top of the fish. Sprinkle salt and pepper on top. Place the fish on a parchment- or foil-lined sheet pan. Place the pan in the oven and cook for 8 to 10 minutes or until the fish is done and flakes easily. Sprinkle additional cilantro on top to garnish.

NOTE: This dish does have a kick to it so use less jalapeño (or none) if you don't want too much spice.

— HOW TO BRING IT —

This is a dish that can be served hot or at room temperature. If you are making it a day in advance, save half of the sauce and the cilantro and add them just before serving to bring a bit of brightness to the fish. If you are planning to reheat the fish, cook it for a shorter time and refrigerate, then reheat from room temperature if possible so you don't overcook it.

The sauce can also be used on almost any protein. If you want, make extra and freeze it for use later on anything from chicken to tofu.

CHAPTER 6

Veggies and Grains

There's no reason for side dishes to get lost in the shuffle. They tend to be simpler and are therefore often easier to make, but that doesn't mean they can't be distinctive. With any communal meal you need to take care of vegetarians who may be attending, and a lot of these dishes can be used as hearty vegetable-based mains. But whether a dish serves as a main or a side, it's all about the flavor.

Veggies and Grains

---◆---

RECIPES

Stuffed Eggplant

There is nothing worse for vegetarians than going to a dinner and realizing that none of the meat-free options qualifies as a main dish. And for meat eaters it's never fun when all the vegetables are a bit too nontraditional. This dish is the perfect meeting in the middle: it is hearty without being heavy, and it can be both main course or side dish. Either way, it's a presentation that everyone will find agreeable.

MAKES 4 SERVINGS

2 small eggplants (preferably the Italian variety)

2 tablespoons extra-virgin olive oil, divided

Salt to taste, divided

2 shallots, diced

2 teaspoons fresh thyme leaves

3 garlic cloves, minced

1/2 cup chopped tomato (fresh or canned is fine)

1/2 cup cooked (or canned) and drained kidney beans

2 tablespoons grated Parmesan cheese

Preheat the oven to 350°F.

Place eggplants on a sheet pan lined with foil, and rub the skins with 1 tablespoon of the olive oil and a dash of salt. Cook for 30 to 35 minutes, turning halfway through until the eggplants have begun to soften and collapse a bit; a knife should slide easily through the eggplants when they are done. If you are using larger eggplants, add at least 10 minutes to the cooking time. Remove from the oven and set aside to cool. Leave the oven on.

Place the rest of the olive oil in a pan on medium-high heat. Add the shallots, thyme, and garlic. Cook for 5 to 7 minutes until the shallots start to brown and look a bit translucent. Cut the eggplants in half lengthwise and carefully scoop out the flesh, leaving the skins intact. Discard the seeds and roughly chop the remaining flesh. Sprinkle salt generously inside the eggplant skins. Add the chopped eggplant, the tomato, and the kidney beans to the shallot mixture. Add a bit more salt and cook for 5 to 7 additional minutes or until the tomatoes are starting to thicken.

Remove the pan from the heat and spoon the contents of the pan into the eggplant shells. Sprinkle Parmesan cheese on top and place back in the oven for an additional 10 minutes. Serve hot or at room temperature.

— HOW TO BRING IT —

This dish does well at room temperature or hot, but if you are aiming to serve it hot, leave the last 10 minutes of cooking until just before you serve it. You can make this dish up to a day ahead. Be sure it has fully cooled down before you store it in a container in the refrigerator.

Zesty Green Beans with Chives

Feeding friends and neighbors shouldn't feel intimidating. Complicated is not always the better choice if you want to impress. The only real goal is to make something delicious. So that's the key with this side dish. It's so simple it may seem like you're hardly even cooking, but the zing you get from the zest and chives makes it feel special.

MAKES 4 SERVINGS

2 lemons

1 pound green beans, trimmed

¼ cup chopped chives

1 tablespoon extra-virgin olive oil

2 garlic cloves, minced

¼ cup blanched slivered almonds

1 teaspoon red pepper flakes

Dash of salt

Zest both lemons, making sure to avoid the white pith. Set the zest aside and juice 1 of the lemons. You should have approximately ¼ cup of lemon juice and 1 tablespoon of zest, but it can be a little more or less.

Bring a large pot of water to a boil and create an ice water bath by filling a large bowl with ice and water. Cook the green beans in the boiling water until they are just cooked but still crisp, approximately 4 minutes. Quickly drain them and submerge them in the ice bath (or run under cold tap water) until they are completely cool. Drain to remove any liquid and add the chives, olive oil, garlic cloves, almonds, red pepper flakes, and salt and toss together. Add the lemon zest and juice just before serving.

— HOW TO BRING IT —

This is another one of those easy-to-prepare gold mines that does well either warm or at room temperature. The key to this dish is the crispiness of the green beans. If you prefer to reheat, cook the green beans a minute or so less when you blanch them. Store the lemon juice and zest separately from the beans, and toss together just before serving.

Spiced-Up Coleslaw

I've been lucky enough to live and travel a lot in Asia, and the most important lesson I try to take with me every day is not to be afraid of bold flavor. This dish is a perfect example of that. Yes, coleslaw is a somewhat ubiquitous and familiar side, but that doesn't mean it has to be boring. You can subtly change the flavors without alienating the traditionalists and make it more exciting for everyone. A coleslaw is just a cabbage salad, and if you skip the mayonnaise-based dressing, it's a blank canvas. With ginger, salt, and zesty lime, this dish is light and fresh and frames cabbage in a whole new way.

MAKES 4 TO 6 SERVINGS

4 cups sliced green or red cabbage (about 1 cabbage)

1 tablespoon red wine vinegar

2 teaspoons finely minced fresh ginger

1½ tablespoons soy sauce

1 tablespoon sesame oil

Juice of 1 lime (about 1 tablespoon lime juice)

½ cup thinly sliced carrots

½ cup thinly sliced scallions

1 cup roasted unsalted peanuts, chopped

Salt to taste

Toss all ingredients in a bowl and taste, adding additional lime juice, salt, or soy sauce as needed. Serve.

— HOW TO BRING IT —

This can hold for up to a day covered in a fridge. Toss well before serving.

Roasted Shaved Squash

There's something fun about changing the typical texture of a piece of produce: it makes you look at it in a whole new light. I love shaved raw squash, but it can also do well if it's cooked. This technique keeps the squash light and crisp and makes it a side dish for any season.

30 MINUTES

MAKES 4 TO 6 SERVINGS

2 pounds yellow squash or green zucchini (or a combination of both)

3 tablespoons extra-virgin olive oil

2 teaspoons coarse salt, plus more to taste

Dash of freshly ground black pepper

1 tablespoon fresh thyme

Grated zest and juice of ½ a lemon

½ cup chopped walnuts

½ cup grated hard sheep's milk cheese such as manchego

Turn on the oven's broiler. Slice the squash with a vegetable peeler or cheese slicer into long strips about ⅛ inch thick. Transfer to a large bowl and toss with the olive oil, salt, pepper, thyme, lemon zest and juice, and walnuts. Spread in a large shallow baking dish and put right under the broiler for 4 minutes, or until the squash is starting to crisp and turn golden. Remove from the broiler. If liquid has collected in the bottom of the dish, drain it off. Sprinkle the cheese over the top and serve.

— HOW TO BRING IT —

This dish can be served hot or at room temperature: try not to serve it stone cold right out of the refrigerator and don't try to reheat it. So much of this dish hinges on the squash being *just* cooked, so if you reheat it, the squash will turn a bit mushy.

Baked Onion

Sometimes the simplest thing can make a meal. For my brother's birthday one year, we went to a fancy restaurant with a set menu where every course was more elaborate than the last, except for one item: baked onions. Unlike the rest of the menu, this dish was completely unadorned, yet it was so flavorful I could barely believe it. When I asked what the secret was, the waiter said that it was baking the onion with the skin on. Sometimes we look past the natural beauty of an ingredient for fussier options, but in the case of the onion, the simplest preparation works like a charm.

MAKES 4 TO 8 SERVINGS

4 yellow onions

½ cup melted butter

Dash of coarse sea salt

Dash of coarse black pepper

Preheat the oven to 400°F. Line a sheet pan with aluminum foil.

Cut the onions in half and trim the tops and bottoms but leave the skins on: be careful to trim only the very tip so as not to lose too much onion or skin. Brush butter all over the onions and place them cut-side up on the sheet pan. Sprinkle with salt and generously crack black pepper on top.

Cook for 60 to 70 minutes, or until the onions are completely tender and have begun to brown. You can serve them in the skin or remove the skin to make them easier to eat—either way discarding the skins.

— HOW TO BRING IT —

These onions are great when hot or at room temperature. They will hold up to 2 days in the fridge if covered properly, but you may want to add a bit more black pepper at the end to enliven their appearance. If you plan to reheat, try to undercook them slightly on first cook: they are pretty forgiving so when you're ready to serve, put them back in the oven (carefully) for 10 to 15 minutes to warm.

Broiled Leeks

The leek is the less-used cousin to the onion, and yet its deep flavor is worth bringing it out of the shadows. This dish gives a bit of char by broiling leeks, and then pairs them with a tangy sauce that livens the whole dish. It's a combination that might encourage people to reconsider leeks.

MAKES 4 TO 6 SERVINGS

6 medium-size leeks

¼ cup Greek yogurt

2 tablespoons fresh lemon juice (about ½ a lemon)

¼ cup chopped parsley

2 garlic cloves, diced

¼ cup very finely diced Granny Smith apple

Dash of salt and freshly ground black pepper

Trim the leeks: cut the green ends off, leaving the paler stalks. Before you trim the roots, wash the leeks thoroughly; if you wash them after cutting off the roots, they will fall apart. Make sure to rinse carefully—the larger the leeks, the sandier they often are. Once all the grit is gone, trim off the root part as well. All that should remain is the white part of the leek.

Place the leeks in a steamer over approximately 1 inch of boiling water. Steam the leeks for 8 to 10 minutes or until they are tender. Cooking time depends on the size of the leeks; don't be afraid to cook them longer if they are larger.

While the leeks are cooking, combine the yogurt, lemon juice, parsley, garlic, and apple in a bowl. The apple should be chopped ultra fine so that big chunks of apple don't overpower the leeks. If you are serving this dish hot, you can microwave the yogurt sauce for 10 seconds to get it to room temperature—but no longer or the yogurt in the sauce will separate. Set the sauce aside.

Turn on the broiler and place a rack in the oven as close to the broiler as possible. Cut the steamed leeks in half lengthwise. Transfer them to a sheet pan lined with aluminum foil, cut-side up, and add a dash of salt and pepper. Set the pan under the broiler for 3 to 5 minutes, or until the leeks start to darken slightly but not burn. Make sure to watch carefully since the line between darkened and burned is very fine.

Remove the pan from the oven, spoon the sauce on top of the leeks, add one more dash of salt and pepper, and serve.

— HOW TO BRING IT —

This dish works fine at room temperature or even cold. You can make it a day ahead but store the sauce and the leeks separately until ready to serve.

Acorn Squash with Parmesan and Hazelnuts

Roasting a big vegetable like a squash can be time consuming, but the result is so flavorful that it's worth the time. Yet in this recipe, you get all of the flavor with less time by cutting the squash into slices. It's a win-win that also means the rich flavor of the caramelized squash doesn't need too many other ingredients to shine.

MAKES 4 TO 6 SERVINGS

5 to 6 pounds acorn squash

2 teaspoons salt

Juice of ½ a lemon

4 tablespoons grated Parmesan cheese

⅔ cup finely chopped hazelnuts

Preheat the oven to 450°F.

Cut the acorn squash in half and scoop out the seeds. Cut the squash into slices, 1 to 2 inches thick: by cutting along the ridges of the squash, you can get even slices. Lay the squash slices on a sheet pan and sprinkle them with salt and lemon juice. Bake for 15 minutes. Sprinkle the Parmesan cheese and hazelnuts on top. Put the squash back in the oven for an additional 5 minutes or until the cheese has melted and started to brown.

— HOW TO BRING IT —

This dish is great hot or at room temperature. If you're making it ahead and want it to be hot, don't add the cheese and hazelnuts until you are ready to reheat and serve: reheated cheese never tastes quite the same.

— SUBSTITUTIONS —

If hazelnuts are hard to find where you are, you can substitute with walnuts.

Squash Bowls

Sometimes you need a dish that is all about the presentation. I'm a sucker for using food as a vessel and this recipe makes an impressive display, adding a festive look to any occasion. There's something about the burnished yellow bowls that always gets people excited. This dish is also notable for its heartiness and works well as a vegetarian main course.

MAKES 4 SERVINGS

4 delicata squash (or another small squash with edible skin)

2 tablespoons extra-virgin olive oil, divided

Dash of salt

1 yellow onion, diced

2 garlic cloves

1/2 teaspoon allspice

1/2 teaspoon cumin

1/2 cup finely chopped parsley

1/4 cup diced Granny Smith apples

Preheat the oven to 400°F.

Cut the 4 squashes in half around the center, leaving 4 small bowl-shaped bottom pieces and 4 more solid top halves. Remove the seeds from the bowl-shaped ends. Cut a thin slice off each bottom half to help it sit level, but take care not to cut off so much that you cut into the bowl. Halve the squash tops, yielding 8 pieces total.

Rub all sides of all the cut squash, including the bowls, with 1 tablespoon of the olive oil and sprinkle all the squash pieces with salt. Place them on a sheet pan and then in the oven for 35 to 40 minutes or until the squash is browned and cooked through.

Set the squash bowls aside. Dice the top quarters of the squash.

Put a skillet over medium-high heat and add the remaining olive oil, onion, and garlic. Cook for 5 to 7 minutes, or until the onion has become translucent and has

(recipe continues)

started to brown. Add the allspice, cumin, parsley, apple, an additional dash of salt, and the diced squash, and cook for another minute, stirring.

Remove this mixture from the heat and spoon it into the squash bowls. Put the bowls back in the oven for 5 minutes to heat through.

— HOW TO BRING IT —

This dish is better when it is warm, so if you make it ahead of time, skip that last reheating. Just before serving, reheat the bowls at 350°F for 5 to 10 minutes to warm through.

Mustard Roasted Carrots

Carrots tend to get short shrift. They are used everywhere from salads to stews, but rarely do they get their own exciting turn. This recipe gives boring old carrots a lift, the mustard providing a piquant counterpoint to the vegetable's subtle sweetness. Carrots also do great at any temperature. Since it works well made ahead of time, it would be an excellent and unusual candidate for a stressful holiday meal.

MAKES 4 TO 6 SERVINGS

2 tablespoons extra-virgin olive oil

2 tablespoons fresh lemon juice (about ½ a lemon)

1 tablespoon Dijon mustard

1 tablespoon whole grain mustard

2 garlic cloves, minced

1 tablespoon fresh thyme

Dash of salt

1 pound carrots, peeled

Preheat the oven to 400°F.

In a bowl, combine the olive oil, lemon juice, mustards, garlic, thyme, and salt. Trim the ends off the carrots and cut them into quarters lengthwise (if they aren't superthick carrots then only cut them in half). Toss the carrots with the seasonings.

Spread the carrots on a sheet pan and place it in the oven. Cook for 30 minutes or so, until the carrots are browning and crisp.

— HOW TO BRING IT —

This dish can be served hot or cold but use restraint in reheating. You can throw them back in an oven at a low temperature to warm, but don't let them get too mushy.

Zucchini and Herbs

I'm kind of a sucker for lots of fresh herbs and lemon on almost anything. A chef friend of mine (and the stylist for all the gorgeous photos you see in this book), Ashton Keefe, wrote an entire book around the idea that the right amount of lemon and salt can transform any dish. Add herbs to that, and I think anything can become a perfect burst of Mediterranean goodness. The seasonings are the important bits here: the zucchini is just the conduit. The amount of zucchini is small, so you are never left with a bite that doesn't feature the star ingredients.

MAKES 4 TO 6 SERVINGS

3 medium zucchinis

½ cup chopped scallions

1 cup halved cherry tomatoes

¼ cup diced shallots

¼ cup chopped basil

¼ cup chopped parsley

¼ cup chopped sage

¼ cup chopped rosemary

Dash of salt and freshly ground black pepper

Juice of ½ a lemon

1 tablespoon extra-virgin olive oil

Turn on your oven's broiler.

Chop the zucchini into small ½-inch matchsticks: the matchsticks don't need to be exactly the same, but the zucchini should, overall, be evenly cut into small bites. Toss the zucchini with the scallions, tomatoes, shallots, basil, parsley, sage, rosemary, salt, pepper, lemon juice, and olive oil.

Pour onto a sheet pan lined with aluminum foil and broil for 4 to 6 minutes, or until the zucchini matchsticks start to brown: you can turn them once to make sure they don't burn. The zucchini should be a bit crunchy.

— HOW TO BRING IT —

This dish tastes great at any temperature. Served hot or cold, it has the same delightful effect. The main thing is to not overcook it: once the zucchini gets too soft, it'll lose some of its punch. Try not to reheat it since it does cook for such a short time.

The Easiest, Nuttiest Creamed Spinach

Creamed spinach is one of those old-school dishes that can ride a fine line between being delicious and an inedible relic. My brother makes fun of me for always trying to update the classics (just leave it alone Ali!), but I knew I was onto something when even he, the lover of all things steakhouse, couldn't stop eating this spinach. Unlike some versions, the goal here is to actually taste the spinach. I also use a bit of cheese with the milk because . . . well . . . doesn't cheese make everything better? The nuts add texture, and I use a shortcut in the form of frozen spinach. It's the most delicious nostalgia, with hardly any heavy lifting.

MAKES 4 TO 6 SERVINGS

4 tablespoons unsalted butter

2 tablespoons all-purpose flour

2/3 cup diced onions (about 1 small to medium onion)

2 garlic cloves, minced or grated

1 cup whole milk

20 ounces frozen spinach, thawed and drained of water in a colander

1/4 cup Parmesan cheese

1/4 cup pine nuts

Dash of salt

Melt the butter in a large saucepan over medium heat and then add the flour and whisk together. Cook for 3 minutes, stirring constantly, until the mixture starts to brown a bit. Add the onion, garlic, and milk, whisking well, and cook another 5 minutes: the flour should dissolve completely with no lumps. Add the spinach and cook for 1 minute to heat through, before taking off the heat. Stir in the cheese, pine nuts, and salt and serve.

— HOW TO BRING IT —

This is one of the few dishes where I would advocate using a microwave to reheat. I would aim not to make this a full day in advance because it will start to congeal and get a bit sad after too much time in the fridge. But if you make it a couple of hours ahead, there is nothing wrong with reheating it in a microwave on a defrosting setting for a few minutes or popping it covered in an oven for a bit to reconstitute itself.

Scallion Quinoa

Whenever my dad wants to make fun of me for being healthy, he always invokes quinoa (pronounced keen-wha for the uninitiated). It's an easy target: it's been used as an example of a miracle grain by everyone from nutritionists to vegans. And while it may not solve all the world's problems, it is a healthy alternative to other more common grains. But being healthy doesn't mean it has to be boring. The joy of quinoa is that it can take on a lot of flavoring. In this recipe it's all about layering flavors. So take a chance on quinoa, even if your more meat-inclined friends might mock you for it initially. They'll be thanking you once they try it.

MAKES 6 TO 8 SERVINGS

2 tablespoons butter or extra-virgin olive oil

1 cup chopped shallots (about 4 to 6 whole shallots)

2 cups chopped scallions, divided

4 cups chicken or vegetable stock (you can also use water if needed, but it won't be as flavorful)

2 cups quinoa (red or white is fine)

2 cups frozen peas

Juice of 2 lemons, divided

1 cup chopped almonds

Salt and freshly ground black pepper to taste

In a pot on medium-high heat, add the butter or olive oil. When the butter melts (or the oil heats up), add the shallots and cook for 3 to 5 minutes, or until they start to soften and brown a bit, stirring occasionally. Add 1 cup of the scallions and cook another 3 to 4 minutes until the scallions have softened as well. Add the stock and bring to a boil. Add the quinoa, the remaining scallions, the peas, and half the lemon juice.

Turn the heat to the lowest setting and cover the pot. Let it cook until all the water is absorbed, approximately 10 to 15 minutes (follow the package instructions). You can stir every 5 minutes or so, but don't check too frequently in the beginning to keep the liquid from evaporating.

When the quinoa seems done, add in the almonds, remaining lemon juice, and salt and pepper to taste, and remove the pot from the heat. Let it sit for a few minutes to finish absorbing the remaining liquid. Stir with a fork to fluff it up.

— HOW TO BRING IT —

Quinoa is pretty forgiving, and it can be served hot or cold. If you're serving it hot, bring the dish to room temperature (if it was refrigerated previously), add a little water, and put it back on the stove or in the oven for a few minutes to heat up. If you are serving it cold, just give it a stir and it should be good to go.

Chickpeas with Chorizo

This is an easy side dish that is packed with flavor. It's so hearty that you may like serving it as a main, with a green salad. I love the spices combined with the chorizo. If you're not familiar with chorizo, it's a dense sausage that is a bit spicy, usually made with ground chili and paprika. If you can't find it, that's okay: any cooked spicy sausage could work here, but try to get something that has a smoky flavor. Served hot or at room temperature, this dish will add a bit of flair to any meal.

MAKES 6 SERVINGS

2 tablespoons extra-virgin olive oil

1 small onion, diced (about 1 cup)

2 cloves garlic, diced

2 tablespoons red wine vinegar

1 teaspoon ground cumin

2 cups cooked or canned chickpeas (about 1½ 15-ounce cans, drained and rinsed)

1 cup diced fresh tomatoes

1 cup diced precooked chorizo (about 5 ounces)

Dash of salt

2 tablespoons chopped parsley

Place a large skillet on medium-high heat. Add the olive oil and onion and cook, stirring occasionally until the onion begins to brown, approximately 5 minutes. Add the garlic, vinegar, cumin, chickpeas, tomato, and chorizo and cook for another 5 minutes: don't stir too often because you want the chickpeas and chorizo to brown. Add a dash of salt (taste to determine, since the chorizo can be salty). Transfer to a serving dish, sprinkle parsley on top, and serve.

— HOW TO BRING IT —

This dish is great warm, but it can also be served at room temperature. The spice tends to bloom after a day in the fridge, so it can be even better if you make it ahead. It travels well and doesn't need a lot of extra fussing to make it work on arrival, although you may want to add the parsley just before serving. If you do reheat, you can do it in a skillet on medium heat or in an oven at 350°F. You can add a dash of water or olive oil to make sure it doesn't dry out. Stir as it cooks again.

Mashed Potato Bake

Mashed potatoes are so simple and yet so satisfying. But they either get relegated to Thanksgiving meals or as a topping for fancier dishes. This dish doesn't play around with too many other flavors: the potatoes get to be the star, with a few other ingredients to bulk it up a bit. It's rustic and simple, but I've seen it become the sleeper hit of the dinner.

MAKES 6 TO 8 SERVINGS

3 pounds russet potatoes (about 6 potatoes)

¼ cup unsalted butter

½ cup diced sage leaves

½ cup diced parsley

½ cup diced shallots (about 2 to 4 shallots)

1 cup heavy cream

2 large eggs, beaten

½ cup grated Parmesan cheese

1 cup frozen peas

1½ teaspoons salt

1 teaspoon freshly ground black pepper

Preheat the oven to 400°F.

Bring a large pot of salted water to a boil. Peel the potatoes, cut them into quarters (or eighths for especially large potatoes), and place them in the pot. Cook for 20 minutes or until the potatoes are fork-tender.

While the potatoes are cooking, melt the butter in a skillet over medium-high heat with the sage, parsley, and shallots. Cook until the butter has fully melted and the shallots have become translucent, approximately 5 minutes.

When the potatoes have finished cooking, drain the water and mash the potatoes until they are almost smooth. I prefer to use a hand masher here rather than a blender because the texture comes out better. Add the butter mixture, heavy cream, eggs, cheese, peas, salt, and pepper to the potatoes and combine fully.

Scoop the mixture into a baking dish and place in the oven for 20 to 25 minutes, until the top has started to brown.

— HOW TO BRING IT —

You can make this recipe ahead of time and just brown in the oven before serving. Plan on needing a bit more time in the oven if the potatoes have been refrigerated. This dish is pretty forgiving so you can travel with it still warm if needed, but it is tastier fresh out of the oven.

Okra in Tomato Sauce

There is a restaurant in Charleston where I grew up that used to make a dish like this, and every time people came to visit I forced them to order it. It was my one trump card when people said they hated okra: it changed their minds every time (except for my mother, who still refuses to accept okra as a viable vegetable). Then one day it disappeared from the menu, and I was left without my okra secret weapon. I had to devise my own version, which luckily still serves the same purpose. The big change I made was that instead of cooking the okra and sauce together, I cook them separately to leave the okra with a nicer texture. Roasting the okra gives it much-needed caramelization, without any mushiness.

MAKES 4 TO 6 SERVINGS

1 pound okra

2 tablespoons extra-virgin olive oil, divided

1 onion, chopped

4 garlic cloves, minced

3 cups chopped fresh tomato

¼ teaspoon chili powder

½ teaspoon paprika

¼ teaspoon allspice

Juice of ½ a lemon

Salt to taste

Preheat the oven to 450°F. Line a sheet pan in aluminum foil.

Trim the okra by cutting off the tips and the stem ends. Toss them in 1 tablespoon of the olive oil, and spread the okra on the prepared pan. Place the pan in the oven and cook for approximately 15 to 20 minutes, or until the okra is tender and has begun to brown (fresher, smaller okra pods take less time to cook). Remove the okra from the oven.

While the okra is baking, set a large saucepan over medium-high heat. Add the remaining 1 tablespoon of olive oil, onion, and garlic and cook for 7 to 10 minutes, or until the onion becomes translucent and starts to brown. Add the tomato, chili powder, paprika, allspice, lemon juice, and salt and cook down until it is a thick sauce, 15 to 20 minutes.

Chop the okra into bite-size pieces (approx-imately ½ to 1 inch) and stir in with the tomato sauce.

— HOW TO BRING IT —

This dish is best hot, but it can easily be briefly reheated because the okra and sauce are very forgiving. Place it back on a stovetop burner, in the oven, or even in the microwave for a few minutes to bring up to temperature.

Couscous with Peas and Onions

Couscous makes a great base because it takes on any flavors you pile into it. It helps hold the dish together and add heft without intruding a lot on the other more exciting ingredients. This is an easy recipe for a picnic or outdoor function because it sits well and doesn't ever quit on you. Think of it as a reliable friend you can always call in a pinch.

MAKES 4 TO 6 SERVINGS

1 large white onion, diced

2 tablespoons salted butter

3 cloves garlic, minced

3/4 cup chicken or vegetable stock, more or less as needed

3 cups frozen peas

1/2 cup couscous

1/3 cup mint

1 tablespoon fresh lemon juice

1/2 cup feta, crumbled

Salt to taste

Put the onion, butter, and garlic in a pot on medium-high heat and sauté for approximately 5 minutes or until the onions start to soften and look translucent. Add the stock, raise the heat to high, and bring to a boil. Add the peas and couscous and immediately remove the pot from the heat. Let stand for 5 minutes. Add the mint, lemon juice, feta, and salt, and fluff the couscous to combine. Cover until it has cooled down significantly, at least 15 minutes, and serve at room temperature or cold.

— HOW TO BRING IT —

This recipe is among the easiest to bring: if you're holding onto it for more than a couple of hours, just make sure to pop it in the fridge, covered. Then take it out when you're ready to serve.

Cauliflower Gratin

Cauliflower has come back into style after years of languishing behind its cousin, broccoli. But while I love the whole roasted cauliflowers that are now so ubiquitous, they aren't easy to share and eat with a crowd. This dish perks up that cauliflower standard but augments it with the all-important element of cheese, along with some fresh herbs.

MAKES 4 TO 6 SERVINGS

1 large head cauliflower, cut into florets

4 tablespoons unsalted butter, at room temperature

½ cup crumbled goat cheese

¼ cup milk

1 garlic clove, minced or grated

2 teaspoons salt

2 teaspoons fresh chopped thyme

2 tablespoons fresh chopped basil

½ cup grated Cheddar cheese

¼ cup breadcrumbs, plain preferred

Preheat the oven to 350°F.

Bring a pot of salted water to a boil and cook the cauliflower florets in the water for 5 minutes or until they have begun to soften but are still firm. Drain the florets thoroughly, and spread them in a large baking dish.

Whisk together the butter, goat cheese, milk, garlic, salt, thyme, and basil. Spread the cheese mixture on top of the cauliflower. Sprinkle with Cheddar cheese and breadcrumbs. Bake in the oven for 15 to 20 minutes or until the topping is brown and bubbling a bit. If it's not browning in your oven, place the dish under the broiler for the last minute or so.

— HOW TO BRING IT —

Any dish with melted cheese is a little sad when completely cold, so while you can make the gratin ahead, do warm it up before serving. Bake it for just 10 to 15 minutes instead of 15 to 20 the first time. If you have refrigerated it, bring it back to room temperature and then pop it back in an oven at 450°F before serving. Don't worry: the extra heat won't overcook the cauliflower. It tastes much better if the cauliflower is a bit crisp inside.

Farro with Charred Vegetables

A hearty grain dish doesn't have to serve up the grains with a heavy hand. Sometimes the extras can have as much heft as the grain itself. This dish works because it breaks down the vegetables to the same size as the farro. You get the nutty flavor and al dente texture of the farro combined with the smokiness of the charred vegetables. It's a winning combination for any season: served hot on a cold evening in, or served cold outdoors at a picnic.

MAKES 4 TO 6 SERVINGS

1 cup semipearled farro

3 garlic cloves, minced

2 cups finely chopped carrots
(the size of farro grains)

3 cups finely chopped broccoli
(the size of farro grains)

1 tablespoon extra-virgin olive oil

Salt to taste, divided

Freshly ground black pepper to taste

½ cup slivered almonds

2 tablespoons cider vinegar

Bring 1½ cups of water to boil in a pot. Add the farro and garlic and then reduce to low heat. Cook for 15 to 20 minutes (or according to the package instructions), until the farro is cooked but still has a bit of texture. When done, remove the pot from the heat, drain any excess water, and let stand to cool off.

While the farro is cooking, turn on your oven's broiler, making sure you have a rack placed close to the heat element. Cover a sheet pan with foil. Place the carrots and broccoli on the pan (but without mixing them together), and drizzle with the olive oil and a sprinkling of salt and pepper. Place them under the broiler for 2 to 4 minutes, or until they start to char but not overcook. You'll want to watch them closely: the difference between a nice char and a burn can happen in a matter of 30 seconds. You may also need to remove the broccoli first and continue cooking the carrots an additional minute or two, depending on how they char.

Once the farro has cooled, add the vegetables, along with the almonds, vinegar, and another dash of salt. Toss to incorporate.

— HOW TO BRING IT —

This dish works if you make it ahead of time and then serve it either hot or cold, but if you are reheating it, try to do it slowly: either covered in the oven or on the stove. You can add a dash of water to reconstitute it as you heat it.

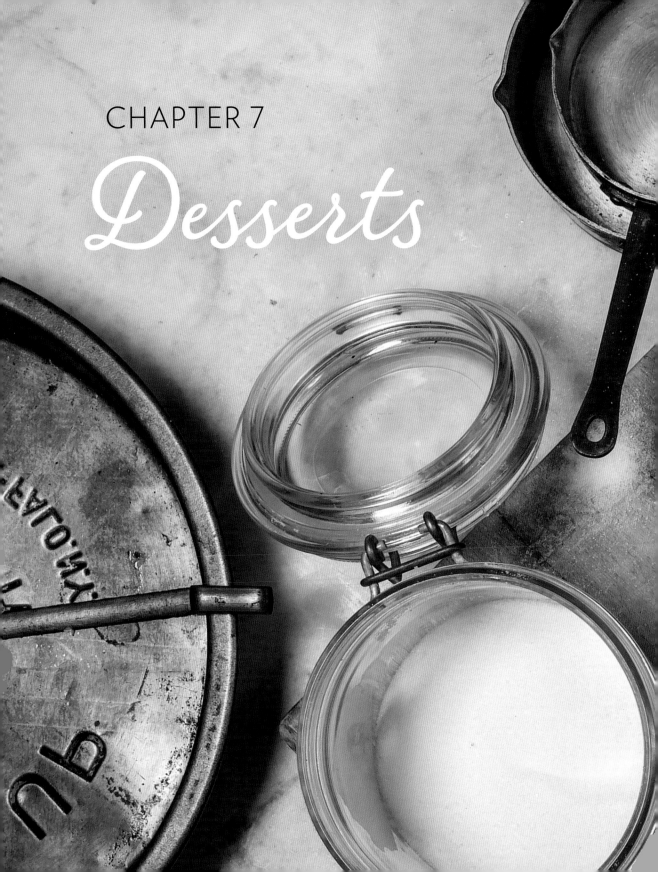

CHAPTER 7

Desserts

After all that choice in appetizers and main courses, you'll have to battle for stomach space if you are bringing dessert. Every recipe in this chapter is a necessary indulgence, no matter how full you think you are. I skipped anything that seemed overly complicated to transport: dishes that have to be served warm are almost completely eliminated here. There's something for the chocoholics, something for fruit lovers, and enough for everyone to wish they had started with dessert.

Desserts

—•—

RECIPES

Berry Crumble

This dessert is basically a cheater's paradise: it looks sort of like a pie, but there's no crust to mess around with. It tastes like you've been baking, but there's nothing that needs to rise. And it's the ultimate substituter's dream: Don't have blueberries? Use blackberries. On top of that, it can be made ahead and served at room temperature. Did I also mention it's delicious?

MAKES 8 SERVINGS

FOR THE FILLING

2 cups fresh blueberries

2 cups fresh strawberries

2 cups fresh raspberries

¼ cup all-purpose flour

¼ teaspoon allspice

¼ teaspoon cinnamon

FOR THE TOPPING

2 cups rolled oats

½ cup all-purpose flour

1 cup dark brown sugar

½ cup salted butter at room temperature, plus additional for buttering the pan

Preheat the oven to 350°F. Butter a 9-inch pie pan.

For the filling, combine the blueberries, strawberries, raspberries, flour, allspice, and cinnamon and place it in a pie pan.

For the topping, combine the oats, flour, sugar, and butter in a separate bowl and stir together: it should resemble a coarse dough. Sprinkle the topping evenly over the filling.

Place in the oven and bake for 40 minutes. Turn the broiler on and broil for 30 seconds to brown the top. Let cool and serve, or refrigerate for up to 2 days before serving.

NOTE: This crumble can handle almost any substitutions. What matters here are the ratios: you want the right filling-to-topping ratio. As long as you use the same amount of fruit, it should all work.

— HOW TO BRING IT —

This dessert works in any configuration from cold to warm: you don't want it to be too hot because then it will be runny. As long as it's covered, you can keep it for a day or two and it will be fine.

Spicy Roasted Pineapple

When I lived in India, one of my favorite things about Indian cooking was the combination of spicy and sweet in many dishes. This recipe is a great unexpected dessert: it takes a fruit that is often just the filler in a fruit salad and makes it into something exciting and different. It also has the benefit of being easy to make and easy to transport. Grilled pineapple is a delight on its own, but by adding a few spicy flavors, you'll make it unforgettable.

MAKES 6 PINEAPPLE SLICES

1 whole pineapple

⅛ teaspoon chili powder or cayenne

2 tablespoons granulated sugar

½ teaspoon ground ginger

Cut up the pineapple: trim the top, bottom, and sides, and then core out the middle (it's also fine to leave the core). Slice the pineapple into 1-inch-thick rounds. In a bowl, mix the chili powder, sugar, and ginger. Sprinkle the chili mixture on top of the pineapple slices.

Place a grill pan on high heat and make sure it has completely reached full heat. Turn on your hood or fan before cooking the pineapple slices, because once they hit the pan they will smoke a bit. Cook the pineapple slices on one side for 2 minutes, without moving them, until the slices have browned. Flip to the other side and repeat. Let them cool on a wire rack, allowing the juice to drip out, before serving them.

— HOW TO BRING IT —

You can make this up to a day ahead, keeping it tightly wrapped in the fridge. Make sure you drain off any excess liquid that accumulates from the slices sitting in the fridge. You can serve it hot off the grill, room temperature, or cold, but don't try to reheat it. You don't want the pineapple to be too soft.

Strawberry Sandwiches

When I first went to Japan I expected all the food to be as composed and refined as we all imagine Japanese food to be. And for the most part it was. But one of my favorite discoveries is that Japan is as bonkers for sandwiches as we are: except that they don't constrain themselves to the savory selection. Everywhere you go during strawberry season, you'll see versions of these simple sandwiches. They might sound completely insane if you've never tried them, but there's something about the combination of sweet strawberries with fluffy white bread and decadent whipped cream that just works. It's like a sandwich version of a strawberry shortcake. Word to the wise here: this recipe is so simple that it lives and dies by its ingredients. So get good strawberries; take the extra minute to make your own whipped cream; and buy the softest white bread you can find. You'll find yourself with an easy-to-serve crowd-pleaser that will delight everyone with its quirkiness.

MAKES 10 TO 12 SANDWICHES

1 cup heavy whipping cream

10 to 12 slices soft white bread (like Wonder Bread)

15 strawberries, chopped into small pieces

Drizzle of honey (optional)

Using a mixer or hand blender (or by hand with a whisk if you have the stamina), whip the cream until it has the texture of whipped cream. The timing will completely depend on what instrument you use, but just watch it carefully to make sure the cream is stiff and holds peaks but is not overwhipped. Cut the crusts off the bread and cut each piece into diagonal halves (or quarters if the bread is on the larger side). Fold the strawberries into the whipped cream. Place a heaping spoonful of the whipped cream and strawberries on top of a slice of bread. Add a small drizzle of honey to the other slice of bread if you'd like your sandwiches a bit sweeter. Put that slice on top and repeat until all the sandwiches have been made. Refrigerate until serving.

NOTE: This recipe is also used in Japan with an abundance of different fruits, so don't be afraid to experiment. Common sandwiches in Japan are kiwi, banana, or blueberry. You can even combine different fruits if you would like. You can also use premade whipped cream if you really need to. It does take away from the freshness of the dish, but in a pinch it will work.

— HOW TO BRING IT —

You want to make these day of because you want the bread to be as fresh as possible. But you can make them up to 6 hours ahead and then cover them tightly before refrigerating.

Baked Pears

My father's favorite dessert has always been poached pears, and they are certainly a classic treat. But they are also a huge pain: you have to painstakingly peel the pears and poach for long hours in a stewing liquid with wine and some spices. Somehow we've convinced ourselves that this is the only way to cook a pear, but the truth is cooked pears are amazing in almost any configuration. This recipe is a standout because it is such a surprising twist on a well-known standard, and it takes way less time to make. Make it ahead or serve it hot, it doesn't matter. The tang of raspberry and the crunch of walnuts will make it memorable no matter how you serve it. There's an important caveat here: try to use the best pears you can possibly find. If the pear wouldn't be delicious (and ripe) before it is cooked then there is no reason it would be great after. With fruit at its peak, you'll have a winning dessert.

MAKES 4 TO 8 SERVINGS

4 medium-sized pears, ripe but not overly ripe (or they will disintegrate)

1/2 cup raspberries

1/4 cup finely chopped walnuts

1 teaspoon honey

1 1/2 teaspoons melted salted butter

2 teaspoons grated lemon zest

Preheat the oven to 400°F. Line a sheet pan with aluminum foil.

Cut the pears in half lengthwise and scoop out the core with a melon baller or carefully with a knife or spoon. Put the raspberries in a bowl and using the back of a spoon smash them up. Add the walnuts, honey, and butter to the smashed raspberries and fully combine. Spread the raspberry mixture on top of the pears on the cut side (you can put a bit of extra mixture in the hole where the seeds were).

Place the pears on the sheet pan with the raspberry side up and place in the oven. Cook for 20 to 30 minutes, depending on the size and ripeness of the pears. They are done when they have softened and browned a bit. Add the lemon zest on top before serving.

— HOW TO BRING IT —

You want to make these day of because you want the bread to be as fresh as possible. But you can make them up to 6 hours ahead and then cover them tightly before refrigerating.

You can serve this dish hot or cold, but if you are going to reheat it, take it out of the refrigerator for an hour before and then heat it up in a 350°F oven for 10 to 15 minutes to bring it back up to temperature. Add the lemon zest right before serving.

— SUBSTITUTIONS —

If you have someone with a nut allergy, this recipe works great with granola substituted for the walnuts. Both are delicious: in recipe testing we went back and forth on which one was better. You can also serve this with whipped cream on top or on the side if you'd like an additional bit of sweetness.

Mango Puff

I relish a heavy dessert as much as the next gal, but sometimes you want light and bright. I have loved the combination of mangoes and coconut ever since I went to Thailand for the first time. This dish will definitely make you feel like you're lying on a tropical beach somewhere. The bonus is that it's easy to make and even easier to serve, all while looking much fancier than it actually is.

MAKES 6 TO 8 SERVINGS

2½ cups diced mango (either fresh or frozen and thawed), divided

1 (14-ounce) can coconut milk

1 teaspoon vanilla extract

Juice of ½ a lemon

1 envelope unflavored gelatin (about 1 tablespoon)

1 cup prepared whipped cream

Mint leaves to garnish

Combine 2 cups of the mango, the coconut milk, vanilla extract, and lemon juice in a blender, and blend until smooth. Set aside.

Boil ¼ cup of water. While the water is coming to a boil, combine ¼ cup of room temperature water with the gelatin. Let it stand for 1 minute to bloom, and then add the boiling water. Stir constantly until the gelatin is completely dissolved. Combine the gelatin with the blended mango mixture until fully incorporated, and then fold the whipped cream into the mixture.

Pour into 6 or 8 ramekins, or small cups if you don't have them. If you don't want to deal with dishes, use clear plastic cups. Add the remaining diced mango on top (make sure they are diced very small so that they don't sink), along with a sprig of mint or chopped mint if you prefer. Cover with plastic wrap and refrigerate for at least 2 hours before serving.

NOTE: The ripeness and variety of mango will alter the sweetness of this recipe. If you have frozen or less sweet mango, you may want to add a tablespoon or so of honey.

— HOW TO BRING IT —

These last in the fridge for at least 3 days as long as they are tightly covered. You can serve these straight out of the fridge, or they can sit out for up to 3 hours before serving. If you are keeping them for more than a day, you may want to add the mango and mint only at the last minute.

Strawberry and Mint Salad

I almost feel like a cheat for calling this a recipe. It's really just combining a couple of things in a bowl and calling it a day. But the result is so delicious and surprising that I think it deserves the status of a recipe. Often people are told to bring a fruit salad, and usually that is a massive disappointment: disparate fruits thrown into a bowl, sitting soggily together, waiting to be eaten. This fruit salad feels purposeful and has some magic to keep it fresh while sitting out. With a little bit of spice, you'll forget that you barely did anything.

MAKES 4 TO 6 SERVINGS

6 cups hulled and quartered strawberries (about 2 pounds)

½ cup finely chopped mint

½ cup chopped walnuts

2 tablespoons granulated sugar

2 teaspoons cider vinegar

2 teaspoons fresh lemon juice

¼ teaspoon ground ginger

Combine all ingredients in a bowl. Serve.

— HOW TO BRING IT —

If the strawberries are going to be waiting more than 2 hours to serve, cover them tightly. You can keep this in the fridge for up to 2 days.

Grilled Peaches with Ricotta

Summertime and grilling are synonymous, but what if you want the grill effect without all the mess? The grill pan is the perfect in-between, and this recipe uses it in the simplest way possible. All it requires is good, juicy peaches: don't try and make this work with the mealy kinds you sometimes get out of season. The rest will speak for itself.

MAKES 10 SERVINGS

5 peaches

2 tablespoons canola oil

2/3 cup ricotta

Drizzle of honey

15 mint leaves, finely chopped

Put a grill pan on high heat (or turn on your grill. You can also use a broiler if you don't have a grill or grill pan). If using a grill pan, make sure to turn on your hood as well. Cut the peaches in half and remove the pits. Brush the cut side of the peaches with canola oil and place them cut-side down on top of the grill pan or grill. Cook them 3 to 4 minutes without moving and then remove. If you are using the broiler, just place them on a sheet pan a few inches from the flame and cook for 3 to 4 minutes.

Add a dollop of ricotta onto each piece (about a spoonful) and drizzle with honey—the amount can vary but keep in mind the more you drizzle, the sweeter the end result. Sprinkle the mint leaves on top.

— HOW TO BRING IT —

This can be made up to a day ahead and stored in the refrigerator tightly wrapped. But it will work best if you grill the peaches and keep the parts separated, drizzling and sprinkling right before serving: it will look much fresher. If you want the peaches hot, you can microwave them for 10 to 20 seconds (depending on how cold they were to start) to get them back up to temperature.

Mini Lemon Meringues

I love a tart dessert, and often I find that when I order them, they are never quite tart enough— always too much cake in the way or not enough zing. This dessert recipe has a lot of words in it that will make you think it is difficult, but that couldn't be further from the truth. These meringues don't need to be perfectly fluffed or piped to work. The curd is simple and foolproof. The meringues are like bites of a homemade candy, and you'll probably be congratulated for not bringing along yet another cake or pie.

MAKES 8 TO 12 MINI MERINGUES

FOR THE MERINGUES

Egg whites from 2 large room temperature eggs

Dash of salt

2/3 cup granulated sugar

1/4 teaspoon ground cloves

1 teaspoon grated lemon zest

FOR THE CURD

3 tablespoons salted butter at room temperature

1/4 cup granulated sugar

1 large egg

Egg yolk from 1 additional large egg

Juice of 2 lemons (about 1/4 cup of lemon juice)

FOR THE GARNISH

8 to 12 blueberries

8 to 12 mint leaves

To make the meringue: Preheat the oven to 275°F. Line a sheet pan with parchment paper, or grease the pan well with oil or unsalted butter.

Beat the egg whites on medium speed in a stand mixer (you can do this by hand but just be prepared to be whisking for a long time!) until they are fully combined, approximately 1 minute. Add the salt, increase the speed to medium high, and add the sugar and cloves slowly, continuously mixing until the egg whites become thick and shiny and hold stiff peaks. They should hold their own shape when you raise the beater; however, this recipe is very forgiving—use your best judgment as to

(recipe continues)

when the whites seem done and it will be fine. Carefully fold in the lemon zest with a spatula.

With a spoon, make disks of the meringue about 3 to 4 inches wide on the prepared sheet pan, with an indent in the middle. You can achieve this by twirling the spoon a full 360 degrees to smooth and even the meringues. You can use a piping bag with a large tip if you want the meringues to look really even but just try not to make them too large. Leave a good amount of space between each one because they spread a bit in the oven. You can make them larger or smaller; just be sure to adjust the cooking time.

Bake for 20 minutes until the meringues are done: they should be hard on the outside but airy and a bit chewy on the inside. Don't overdo it. If the meringues are dry and crisp all the way through—they are overdone—so check often! Cool the pan on a rack when done.

To make the curd: Beat the butter and sugar together with a mixer. Add in the egg and yolk, one at a time, still mixing slowly. Add the lemon juice and mix again until it all combines. Set a saucepan over low heat and add the lemon mixture. Stir constantly until the mixture thickens, approximately 10 minutes. It should never boil or quite simmer. When thick enough (like the texture of a thick pudding), take off the heat to cool.

Once both the meringues and the curd have sufficiently cooled, spoon the curd on top of each meringue and smooth out. Place a mint leaf and a blueberry on top of each one.

NOTE: I hate to force people to buy a new spice for just a 1/4 teaspoon, so if you need to replace the cloves with cinnamon or allspice, do so. But I will say that on every test, clove was the most beloved ingredient. You can also garnish as you see fit with almost any kind of fruit, or just use a slice of lemon zest on top.

— HOW TO BRING IT —

This is a great dish for making ahead but try to keep all the parts separate until a few hours before serving. Store the meringues in an airtight container and keep the curd refrigerated. Because this dessert assembles quickly, you can put it all together at your destination.

Goat Cheese Pumpkin Pie

Pumpkin pie is one of those great things that let you know fall has arrived, but it can still bring joy to any season. This version adds a depth of flavor with the goat cheese. It's also one of the easiest pies to make. You don't need any special equipment, although if you want to make it more elaborate you could start with fresh pumpkin: just be sure to buy one of the small varieties that are best for pies (sugar pumpkins are my favorites) and roast it in the oven at 350°F for 30 to 45 minutes until soft. Pumpkin pie also has the advantage of taking on whatever seasonal toppings you'd like. I've done everything from fresh cranberries to pecans.

MAKES 8 TO 10 SERVINGS

1 pie crust (store bought or page 119)

1 (14-ounce) can pumpkin purée (100% pure pumpkin)

½ cup cream cheese

8 ounces goat cheese

½ teaspoon allspice

1 teaspoon vanilla extract

½ teaspoon cinnamon

½ teaspoon grated fresh ginger

½ cup granulated sugar

½ cup dark brown sugar

4 eggs

¼ teaspoon salt

Preheat the oven to 350°F.

Place the pie crust in a pie pan and crimp the edges. Bake the pie crust for 5 to 7 minutes, until it has started to harden but not yet brown. Remove it from the oven and cool.

Stir together the pumpkin, cream cheese, goat cheese, allspice, vanilla extract, cinnamon, ginger, sugars, eggs, and salt in a bowl. Spread the mixture into the cooled pie crust and bake for 30 to 40 minutes, until the crust has started to brown and the center of the pie is still a little jiggly (it will firm up once removed from the heat so you don't want it to be overdone). Cool and serve.

— HOW TO BRING IT —

This can be made up to 2 days ahead: just wrap loosely in foil without it touching the pumpkin filling.

Strawberry Rhubarb Pie

A pie is like a potluck secret weapon. Unlike fussier desserts, a pie can always fit with the theme of the evening, whether it's a casual night in or a larger dinner party. This pie has undeniably delicious flavors. It's literally the pie my grandmother used to make and one I would look forward to on every visit. And even though in my mind, it's inseparable from my strong memory of her, it's hard for anyone not to like this pie. This pie relies on rhubarb being in season; I always had this with rhubarb fresh from my grandmother's New Hampshire garden in the summer, and there's nothing like peak season ingredients. But in a pinch you could make it with frozen and thawed rhubarb as well. It's the kind of recipe where the combination is great no matter what. It isn't too sweet, it isn't too heavy, and one slice just isn't enough.

MAKES 8 SERVINGS

2½ cups sliced strawberries

1½ cups sliced fresh rhubarb

½ cup granulated sugar, divided

2 pie crusts (store bought or page 119)

1 teaspoon grated lemon zest

1 teaspoon fresh lemon juice

2 tablespoons all-purpose flour

Very small pinch of salt

Combine the strawberries and rhubarb in a bowl. Toss with half of the sugar, and set the fruit in a colander over a bowl to drain for 1 hour.

Preheat the oven to 400°F. Move the oven rack into the lower third of the oven.

If using a homemade pie crust, roll out one crust and place it in an 8- or 9-inch pie pan, overhanging the sides. Roll out the second crust and cut it into 1-inch strips.

Place the drained fruit in a clean bowl and add the remaining ¼ cup of sugar, lemon zest and juice, flour, and salt. Toss to combine.

Fill the prepared pie shell with the fruit mixture. Top with a lattice crust, or a crust of your choosing. If you want to make the lattice

(recipe continues)

crust, lay down the vertical strips evenly across your pie. Then fold back every other strip and place a horizontal strip down. Fold the vertical strips back down. Now unfold the opposite strips over a second strip. Repeat until the lattice is complete: you should have an equal number of strips vertically and horizontally that weave over and under each other.

Set the pie on a sheet pan lined with aluminum foil (to catch any spills), and bake the pie for about 35 minutes. If the edges of the pie are browning too much, cover with a foil ring. Continue to bake the pie for about another 10 minutes or until the crust is a golden-brown color and the fruit juices begin to bubble through the center. Remove the pie from the oven and place on a wire rack to cool.

— HOW TO BRING IT —

Pies are great served hot, but they actually need a bit of resting time to come together. You can certainly make this pie and then put it back in the oven for a few minutes to get it warm, but it doesn't necessarily need it.

Brown Butter Pie

Once you begin making brown butter, it is fairly addictive. The nutty aroma completely changes the butter we know and love. This recipe is based on one of the most decadent Southern desserts around called chess pie. Instead of trying too hard to improve what works, this focuses on the good stuff: butter, sugar, cream, and eggs. You're left with a pie that is simple in preparation but a true showstopper.

MAKES 6 TO 10 SERVINGS

1 pie crust (store bought or page 119)

½ cup unsalted butter

1 cup granulated sugar

¼ cup dark brown sugar

1 teaspoon salt

4 large egg yolks

1 teaspoon vanilla extract

⅓ cup heavy whipping cream

1 teaspoon grated lemon zest

Confectioners' sugar for dusting

Preheat the oven to 350°F, making sure the rack is in the center of the oven.

Place the pie crust in a pie pan and crimp the edges. Refrigerate the pie pan until ready to use.

In a pan on medium heat, melt the butter and allow it to brown. The butter will foam a bit and then start to turn golden: make sure to stir continually as it browns, removing from the heat immediately once it is caramel colored with a nutty aroma. If the milk solids at the bottom start to blacken, you'll want to start over because all of it will taste burned.

Set the butter aside to cool. Once the butter has cooled a bit, add both sugars and the salt and whisk until fully combined. Add the egg yolks, vanilla, cream, and lemon zest, and whisk again until blended. Pour the filling into the pie crust.

Bake the pie for 40 to 45 minutes or until it has browned and is set around the edges but the center is still a bit jiggly. Remove the pie from the oven and let it cool to room temperature. Refrigerate for at least 5 hours before serving. Dust with confectioners' sugar before serving.

— HOW TO BRING IT —

This dish should be made ahead because it needs to refrigerate. You can make it up to 2 days before serving, just keep it covered and chilled.

Tarte Tatin

This is a classic, rustic French tart that my mother-in-law introduced me to, and I have been making it ever since. Unlike a lot of desserts, it isn't about precision and looking put-together. On the contrary, tarte tatin is meant to look a little shiny and browned around the edges. But it has its own beauty and is extremely forgiving. It is also, luckily, extremely delicious. The key here is to be patient: don't worry about whether it is cooking properly and start to fuss over it. This is a dish that when left to its own devices takes one ingredient and almost magically turns it into something else. The caramelized sugar on the apples is delicious enough that you don't need more than four simple ingredients.

MAKES 8 SERVINGS

7 to 8 large apples with a firm texture, such as Gala, Braeburn, Honeycrisp, or Granny Smith (you can also mix and match)

¼ cup unsalted butter, at room temperature

¼ cup granulated sugar

1 puff pastry sheet (about 8 to 10 ounces)

At least 1 day before making the tart, peel, core, and quarter the apples. Leave them in a bowl covered with a paper towel to dry out. Don't worry: they *will* get brown, but it won't matter once you cook them.

Once your apples are ready, preheat the oven to 400°F.

Heat a skillet on medium heat and melt the butter in the pan. Sprinkle the sugar evenly over the butter. Place the apples in tight concentric circles around the pan, starting from the center. Don't worry if the placement isn't perfect since the apples will cook down: it never feels even or correct, and that's okay. The key is just to make sure there is no space in between the apples. Let the apples cook undisturbed for 15 minutes until the juices start to brown.

Place the pastry sheet on top of the apples, making sure to tuck the sides down into the pan. Place into the oven and cook for 25 to 30 minutes until the pastry has browned. Remove from the oven and let cool for at least 10 minutes.

Run a sharp knife around the edge of the pastry to loosen it from the pan. Carefully (very carefully!) hold a plate upside down over the pan with both hands, flush against the pastry, and invert the tart onto the plate so that the apples are now facing up. If any of the apples stick to the pan just scrape them out and place them on top. Serve.

— HOW TO BRING IT —

Tarte tatin can be served at room temperature if it is served within 6 hours, but if you are making it a day ahead of time (or in the morning for an evening event), be sure to reheat it a bit so that the caramel melts again. You can place it on a tray in an oven at 300°F for 5 or 10 minutes, or you can even microwave it for a minute in a pinch. Just don't overdo it: you don't want to lose the texture.

Caramel Pie Bars

Marlene Koch, the author of the bestselling Eat What You Love *series, insisted to me that no book of totable recipes could exist without a pie bar. And she was absolutely right: they are so much easier to eat in a group than cake or a slice of pie, but they have more going on than a cookie. This particular pie bar is uber-sweet and unapologetic about it. Caramel can sound daunting, but it is actually among the simplest items to make: water and sugar come together to make something rich and delicious.*

MAKES 8 TO 12 PIE BARS

FOR THE CRUST

¼ cup granulated sugar

¼ cup brown sugar

½ teaspoon salt

¾ cup salted butter, at room temperature

1½ cups all-purpose flour

FOR THE CARAMEL

¾ cup granulated sugar

¼ cup heavy cream

1 teaspoon vanilla extract

FOR THE FILLING

⅔ cup brown sugar 2 eggs

1 cup coarsely chopped pecans or chocolate chips (or a combination!)

Preheat the oven to 350°F. Grease the bottom and sides of a 13 x 9-inch pan with cooking spray or butter or line with greased aluminum foil if you prefer.

Start with the crust: In a bowl, mix the sugars, salt, and butter together and then carefully stir in the flour, taking care to not overmix. When the mixture resembles a dough, place it at the bottom of the pan and press it in so that it evenly covers the whole bottom. Bake for 15 to 18 minutes until the edges have started to brown. Remove from the oven and let it cool (the mixture might still be a bit soft, but after 5 minutes of cooling it should firm up a bit).

While the crust is baking, make the caramel. In a deep pan on medium heat, combine ¼ cup of water and the sugar. Stir until the sugar has dissolved and the mixture comes to a boil: be careful not to rush it; it should take about 3 to 4 minutes. Turn down the heat enough so that the mixture is simmering instead of boiling and let it cook for 5 to 7 more minutes. You'll want to swirl the pan around and watch carefully. It should become a medium amber color. Add the cream and vanilla (watch for splatters as it bubbles up), bring back up to a low simmer, and then stir consistently for 3 more minutes until it has reduced a bit more. Remove from the heat and pour the caramel into a bowl. Let it cool for at least 5 minutes. The consistency should be syrupy but still loose.

In a separate bowl combine the brown sugar and eggs. Add the caramel and stir until completely combined. Pour the caramel mixture on top of the crust. Sprinkle the pecans or chocolate chips on top. Place in the oven for 25 to 30 minutes, or until the bars have completely set. Remove from the oven and let cool completely, at least 30 minutes. Remove from the pan and cut the bars to a size of your preference.

— SUBSTITUTIONS —

The top of the caramel bar is really up to interpretation. I have made them with both pecans and chocolate, and no one could ever agree which was the favorite, so I've included them both. But you can also add other toppings: different kinds of nuts, brown sugar, or other chocolate candies could also work. The only one I would caution against adding is caramel candies: it really is too much.

— HOW TO BRING IT —

The pie bars can be stored covered in a fridge for up to 2 days, but try to not cut the bars until at least a few hours before serving.

Chocolate Sesame Truffles

There are few things as widely beloved as a ball of chocolate. But you can have too much of a good thing, and these truffles find the right balance, with decadent dark chocolate rounded out with the nutty flavor of sesame seeds. They are also super easy to make. Unlike a lot of truffle recipes, this one doesn't require a bunch of steps or double boilers. It may not look quite as nice to begin with, but once you roll them in the sesame seeds, they'll look like a professional made them. It's a quick turnaround for a dessert that is easy to serve and even easier to eat.

MAKES 15 TO 20 SMALL TRUFFLES

⅓ cup heavy cream

3 ounces bittersweet chocolate (70%), broken or cut into small pieces

⅓ cup cocoa powder

1 tablespoon butter

3 tablespoons tahini

¼ cup sesame seeds, more or less as needed

Place a saucepan on high heat and bring the heavy cream to a boil. Turn the heat off and add the chocolate, cocoa powder, and butter. Stir until the chocolate and butter have melted. Stir in the tahini and place in the freezer for 15 to 20 minutes, stirring every 5 minutes. You can leave it in the saucepan if you have room in your freezer or transfer to a bowl. The mixture should have firmed up enough to be rolled into balls. If it isn't, stir it again and leave it in for another 5 minutes. Roll the truffles into small balls, coating with the sesame seeds. Refrigerate until 5 to 10 minutes before serving.

— HOW TO BRING IT —

These do great refrigerated for up to 2 days as long as they are tightly covered.

Chocolate and Walnut Rice Krispies Bars

I know Rice Krispies treats might seem like a basic dessert, but if you haven't tried this spiced-up version then you really don't know what you're missing. I made this dish for a big group where everyone insisted on having backup treats without the walnuts. By the end of the night the skeptics were raving about the nuttiness and texture that the walnuts give to the dish. The classic version is the ultimate anytime dessert: they keep well, they are easy to portion, and everybody loves them— but with this twist you'll have a lot of people suddenly rethinking the old favorite.

MAKES 8 TO 12 SERVINGS

5 tablespoons salted butter, plus additional for greasing the pan

¼ cup unsweetened chocolate chips or 1 unsweetened chocolate bar (about 2 ounces), broken into small pieces

1 (10-ounce) package mini marshmallows

2 tablespoons cocoa powder

1 teaspoon fresh orange juice

6 cups crisp cereal (Rice Krispies preferred)

1 cup chopped walnuts

Grease a baking dish with butter. Melt the butter and unsweetened chocolate in a large saucepan on medium heat, stirring throughout. Once they have melted and are smooth, add in the marshmallows, cocoa powder, and orange juice, stirring frequently until the marshmallows are also melted. The timing on this will vary depending on your heat and the type of marshmallows, but you should be watching it and stirring it constantly so it doesn't overcook. Turn off the heat and fold in the cereal and walnuts. Spread into the pan while still warm, smoothing the top and sides with a spatula. Let the mixture sit at least 30 minutes before cutting into squares and serving.

— HOW TO BRING IT —

In an airtight container these can hold for up to 3 days. You can also make them into balls instead of squares if you want to do something smaller or a little different; just make sure to shape them while they are warm and spray your hands with cooking spray, or use a bit of softened butter.

— SUBSTITUTIONS —

This dish needs the nuts—trust me, in a group of walnut haters it still won the day—but you can replace the walnuts with cashews, pecans, or other nuts. If you really aren't going to take my advice or someone has a serious nut allergy, try adding in a tablespoon of orange zest to give the dish a little something to cut through all the chocolate.

S'mores Bars

Much as I would like to, it's not practical to have a campfire in the middle of your home (we can dream though, right?). This dessert takes classic flavors and makes them portable. The s'mores bars are like condensed little campfire treats that are also pretty simple to make. I take the path of least resistance here: there's no premelting or overly complicated scenarios. Just layer the ingredients on top of one another, and leave carrying the firewood to someone else.

MAKES 8 TO 10 SERVINGS

3 cups crushed graham crackers

2/3 cup dark brown sugar

1/2 cup salted butter, melted, plus additional for the pan

1 egg, beaten

1 cup semisweet chocolate chips

2 cups mini marshmallows

Preheat the oven to 350°F. Grease a baking pan, approximately 13 x 9 inches.

Stir the crushed graham crackers, brown sugar, butter, and egg together until fully incorporated. Spread the mixture across the baking pan. Bake it in the oven for 15 minutes, until the crust is firm.

Remove the pan from the oven and sprinkle the chocolate chips and marshmallows evenly over the crust. Return to the oven to bake for 10 more minutes, and then turn on the broiler and broil for an additional 30 seconds to 1 minute, making sure to brown but not burn the top.

Remove and allow to fully cool to at least room temperature. Cut into squares before serving.

— HOW TO BRING IT —

This dessert can be made up to 2 days ahead, covered and refrigerated, but try not to cut it until the day you are serving it.

Chai Brownies

I probably drank a few thousand cups of chai when I lived in India. Everywhere you go you'll find the spicy tea. Every combination is different, but it was always the cardamom that did it for me. I discovered that adding a bit of that flavor to ordinary brownies makes them richer and more delectable. It's a small addition, but the cardamom, along with the fudge-inducing brown sugar, makes a world of difference.

MAKES 8 BROWNIES

8 tablespoons unsalted butter, cut into tablespoons

3 ounces bittersweet chocolate, broken into pieces

3/4 cup granulated sugar

1/4 cup light brown sugar

2 large eggs, beaten

3/4 cup flour

1/2 teaspoon salt

1/4 teaspoon vanilla extract

1/4 teaspoon ground cardamom

1/4 teaspoon ground cloves

Preheat the oven to 350°F. Line a baking pan with foil and spray it with a nonstick spray. (You can spray or butter your pan without the foil as well, but it makes it a bit easier to get the brownies out.)

Place a saucepan on low heat and add the butter and chocolate. Stir constantly until the butter and chocolate have melted. Remove from the heat, wait a minute, and add the granulated and brown sugars. Make sure the sugars are incorporated and then slowly add the eggs, whisking as you go. Add the flour, salt, vanilla, cardamom, and cloves and stir gently: don't overstir but make sure all the ingredients have combined.

Pour the batter into the pan and bake for 20 to 25 minutes. You can stick a toothpick in the center to make sure it comes out clean, but start checking earlier rather than later. Brownies will continue cooking once removed from the oven, and you don't want them to be too dry. Let them cool and then remove from the pan and cut into squares.

— HOW TO BRING IT —

Brownies can be made 2 days in advance and stored in plastic wrap or foil (cool before wrapping). You can keep them in the fridge but make sure to serve them at room temperature (or a bit warmed).

Peanut Butter Cheesecake Cupcakes

This recipe's name is a mouthful—for a dessert that's a mouthful of goodness. The creamy texture of cheesecake and peanut butter blend perfectly. And by making them into little cupcakes, you have single-serve desserts that delight a crowd. These mini cakes are light compared to traditional cheesecake but serious enough to make dessertaholics happy.

MAKES 16 CHEESECAKE CUPCAKES

1½ cups finely crumbled graham crackers

⅓ cup dark brown sugar

3 tablespoons butter, melted

1 pound (16 ounces) cream cheese, at room temperature

¼ cup granulated sugar

2 teaspoons vanilla extract

1 cup peanut butter, at room temperature

½ cup heavy cream

2 eggs

⅔ cup chocolate chips

Preheat the oven to 300°F. Place paper liners in a muffin tin.

In a bowl, combine the graham cracker crumbs with the sugar and butter. Press the mixture down into each of the cupcake liners to form a bottom crust.

In the bowl of a stand mixer, combine the cream cheese, sugar, and vanilla extract and beat well. Add the peanut butter and heavy cream and beat again until fully incorporated: this could take a bit longer if the peanut butter doesn't incorporate easily or if it's cold. Add the eggs and then mix again until just combined.

Spoon the cheesecake mixture on top of the crusts. Sprinkle the chocolate chips on top. Bake 20 to 25 minutes or until the cheesecake has set. Remove and cool for at least 2 hours in the fridge before serving.

— HOW TO BRING IT —

These mini cheesecakes store well for up to 2 days in the fridge as long as they are tightly covered: you can use foil or plastic wrap.

Snowy Chocolate Cookies

The inside of a cookie is what counts, but you can't ignore the visual aspect. A cookie that has that extra spark always wins the day. I learned this trick of rolling cookies in confectioners' sugar from Milk Bar guru Christina Tosi. The effect is a stunning crackled look, and the sugar adds a bit of extra sweetness. This cookie is a chocolate lover's dream. Anyone who isn't a true chocoholic might want to stay away because these cookies are crumbly balls of chocolate intensity. Every event needs one major chocolate contribution, and this is it.

MAKES 12 COOKIES

9 ounces bittersweet chocolate,
 broken into pieces

½ cup all-purpose flour

¼ cup unsweetened cocoa powder

¼ teaspoon baking soda

¼ teaspoon salt

4 tablespoons unsalted butter,
at room temperature

¼ cup light brown sugar

¼ cup granulated sugar

2 large room temperature eggs

½ cup confectioners' sugar

Place the chocolate in a saucepan on medium heat and stir constantly until fully melted. Set aside to cool.

Sift the flour, cocoa powder, baking soda, and salt together and set aside. Combine the butter, brown sugar, and granulated sugar together in a stand mixer and beat until fluffy, about 3 minutes (you can beat by hand but be sure to combine until very fluffy). Add the eggs one by one while the mixer runs on a low speed, and then add the melted chocolate.

Once combined, slowly add the flour mixture, making sure to combine fully but not to overmix. Wrap the dough in plastic wrap and chill it for at least an hour (you can keep it in the fridge for up to 24 hours like this).

Once the dough has cooled, preheat the oven to 350°F. Line a sheet pan with parchment paper or spray with nonstick cooking spray.

Roll the dough into balls and then lightly roll the balls in the confectioners' sugar until they are completely coated. Place the dough balls on the prepared sheet pan, leaving at least an inch between each one. Bake for 12 to 14 minutes, or until they have cooked but are still a little soft and then remove them from the oven: they will seem underdone but they will firm up as they cool. Cool for at least 15 minutes before serving.

— HOW TO BRING IT —

These cookies need to be handled with care because they are supposed to be on the softer side, so don't toss them around the way you would a crunchier cookie. They can be stored for up to 2 days in an airtight container, and they'll do just fine. You can also keep the dough frozen for up to two months: just make sure you defrost in the fridge for a day before making them.

Spice Cookies

Hands down my favorite baker is Dorie Greenspan, but she and I once had a philosophical disagreement about whether crunchy cookies or soft cookies were better. She wouldn't admit that soft cookies are better (they are), but she did, however, give me a genius tip for spice cookies. Let your spice cookies sit—either the dough, before you bake them, or the baked cookies—because it helps the spiciness develop. These cookies are great either way, with the fresh ginger making them come alive even if you eat them right out of the oven, but I'd stick with Dorie's tip and give them some time to bloom.

MAKES 8 TO 12 COOKIES

2 cups all-purpose flour

1 teaspoon baking soda

1/4 teaspoon ground cloves

1/4 teaspoon allspice

1/4 teaspoon cinnamon

1/2 cup molasses

1 teaspoon scraped seeds from a vanilla bean (or substitute 2 teaspoons vanilla extract)

11/2 teaspoons fresh grated ginger

1 egg

1 cup dark brown sugar

1/2 cup salted butter, at room temperature

Grated zest from 1 orange

Preheat the oven to 375°F.

In a bowl combine the flour, baking soda, cloves, allspice, and cinnamon. In the bowl of a stand mixer combine the molasses, vanilla, ginger, egg, brown sugar, and butter and beat on low speed until it is a bit fluffy (this can be done by hand but do get it really fluffy). Add the flour mixture and slowly combine, making sure not to overmix.

Line a sheet pan with parchment paper (or you can grease it with melted butter) and scoop out the dough into balls with a cookie scoop if you have it, or an ice cream scoop or large spoon; just make sure they are uniform. Bake for 10 to 12 minutes, rotating halfway through, or until the cookies are browned a bit but still soft.

Note that these cookies will seem too soft but they firm up a bit once they cool, so don't be afraid to take them out. Place them on a cooling rack or remove them from the pan to cool. Sprinkle the orange zest over the top, and if possible, let the cookies rest for a few hours or a day before serving.

— HOW TO BRING IT —

As mentioned above, these get even better in the spice department after a day, so feel free to make them ahead. Just be sure to store them in an airtight container.

ACKNOWLEDGMENTS

This book was a true labor of love. It was created over meals with my siblings in my tiny New York kitchen; in my parents' home in Charleston; and at friends' houses who were game to try out untested ideas and allow for a few failures (shout-out to Emily and Marco for suffering through the world's spiciest pineapple disaster and my in-laws for gracefully attempting to eat a misguided modernized tuna casserole). I had such a supportive network, and this small, back-of-the-book thank you will never be enough gratitude.

I have to start with thanks for my incredible agent Sharon Bowers, who got me from the moment we met and answered every possible inane question from a first-time author. And mostly for connecting me to my wonderful editor Kristen Green Wiewora. It's the dream to get an editor who somehow can rework your writing to make you sound like a better version of yourself. Thanks for putting up with me and letting me bounce any idea off you no matter how nutty. The whole Running Press team has been incredible.

Visually, this book has a dream team. Susan Van Horn is a designer with an eye like a laser. Kristi Hunter prop styles like a ninja—moving a teaspoon ever so slightly to somehow make it all come together. Noah Fecks (and his right hand Christopher Rogers) took such incredible photos, which brought these recipes to life, and let us all have a blast doing it. Caroline Verrone is a whiz in the kitchen. And to my partner in bread and booths, Ashton Keefe: you are the kindest soul who also just happens to be the best in the business at pretty much everything you do. This group of people blew me away, and I hope the fun we had shooting this book comes through in the photos.

I also cannot thank my recipe testers enough. I put out a call for home cooks to test, and friends and family from all over the country enthusiastically volunteered. My goal was for every recipe to work in every kitchen, and by having this network of cooks, I believe they helped achieve that. Thank you Elizabeth Allen, Lynn Reisman, Tina Clabbers, Jennifer Baum, Benn Waters, Juliet Izon, Claire Reyner, Tara Hohenberger, Sarah Ruderman, Linnea Covington, Jessica Leibowitz, Rachel Shelasky Kerasik, Tia Keenan, Mary-Louise Ramsdale, Karen Moore, Alana Rush, and

Mari Ono (and my permanent tasters, Pia, Alana, and Blaske, along with Carly, Jane, Jess, and Marcy for awards show bonanzas). And Ellie Bernal (for everything).

I had a lot of cookbook writers give me great advice to help me learn from their experiences, so thanks for taking the time Kate Heddings, Farideh Sadeghin, Marlene Koch, Jamie Feldmar, Katie Parla, and Serena Wolf. Dorie Greenspan is also the best FaceTime coffee date a girl could ask for.

Thank you to the teachers in my life. Our life's work stands on the shoulders of all the people who devoted their lives to teaching, and I had some of the best. Particular thanks to Sharon Leff, Catherine Tousignant, and Seth Bardo who unflinchingly (and, dare I say, gleefully?) tore apart all my essays and forced me to stop being such a terrible writer.

My beloved mother-in-law, Rachel, passed away while I was writing this book, and I am devastated she will never get to hold a finished copy because she has taught me so much about not only cooking but how to truly host and care for people. I feel grateful that she got to read the dedication and know how much of her went into this book. And to my father-in-law, Yehuda, whose strength gives me strength and who graciously allowed me to use his glorious kitchen for the photo shoot. And to Natalie, Aaron, and Leo for being the other part of my heart right upstairs.

Thank you to my siblings and their significant others for being the true taste of this book. Annie, Will, Jon, and Skye—I really, honestly, could not have done this without our Thursday night dinners. I am the luckiest girl in the world to have siblings who double as best friends, and I will never take that for granted. It's a gift that I am grateful for every day.

To my son, Guy, for being the absolute light of my life (cheesy for sure, but true).

Thank you to my husband, Daniel, who has also gleefully torn up my writing from time to time to make it infinitely better. He not only came up with the title for this book (credit where credit is due), but he has been willing to let me walk my own path since the day we met at the age of nineteen.

Lastly, and most importantly, thank you to my parents. My dad is the best writer that I know. And I'm really proud that everyone in my family calls me "Susan Junior." All my life you've allowed me to explore when other parents would have said no. I can never thank you enough for everything you've done for me.

INDEX

Note: Page references in *italics* indicate photographs.